The Dow Twins' Legacy

50 YEARS OF DISCO REFLECTIONS

BY HAROLD A. DOW

The Dow Twins' Legacy: 50 Years of Disco Reflections

Copyright © 2024, Harold A. Dow
tennisbum620@gmail.com

All rights reserved. No part of this book may be used or reproduced by any means, graphic, electronic, or mechanical, including photocopying, recording, taping or by any information storage retrieval system without the written permission of the author except in the case of brief quotations embodied in critical articles and reviews.

Cover Design and Interior Typeset by Iryna Spica, irynaspicabookdesigner.ca

ISBNs:

Hardcover - 979-8-218-35748-1

D.T. Media Group, Ltd
P.O. Box 340301
Queens, NY 11434-9997

*In memory of my parents,
Evelyn and Reginald N. Dow,
his father Arthur Dow,
and her mother Francis Sims,
who happily spoiled us.*

*To my twin brother, Norman,
who was generous to a fault, loving,
and the best partner ever.*

*To Uncle Dave and Aunt Vivian,
who tried to expose us to all the cultural
activities in New York City.*

*And to all those
who were so encouraging over the years
as I worked on this project,
even after the death of my brother:
this book is dedicated to you.*

Table of Contents

Acknowledgements ix
Foreword xv
Introduction xxiii

1. How It All Began 1
   Childhood 4
   Surviving St. John's. 14

2. Never Let Them See You Sweat 27
   The Move to Manhattan 28
   The Best of Friends: Leviticus, Othello and Justine's. 34

3. The Formula For Bringing People Together 63
   Manhattan Proper Café 63
   The WWRL Years. 79
   The U.S.S. Intrepid and Copacabana 90

4. Giving People a Reason to Be Cheerful. 115
   The Dow Twins' 20th Anniversary Gala 115
   The Formula for Long-Term Success 124
   So Many Reasons to Be Cheerful 135

5. Building the Brand 151
   Salsa Fridays After Work at Justine's 156
   The South Street Seaport 157

      A Day at the Races 160
      The MASKquerade Balls 162
      Gemini & Cancer Birthday Celebrations 165
      Tian at the Riverbank Grill Restaurant. 165

6. The Sports We Loved .173
      Bowling 174
      Tennis 175
      Skiing. 179
      Spectator Sports: Formula One Racing. 194
      Spectator Sports: The New York Mets and
      the New York Giants 197

7. Friends & Lovers 201
      Love and The Dow Twins. 202
      Norman 205
      Harold 217
      Les Amies 221
      I Met My Spouse at a Dow Twins' Event 227

8. Giving Back to the Community 237
      Dow Scholarships 238
      Supporting Non-Profits 243

9. Epilogue—Moving On. 253
      Condolence Messages for Norman 257
      Norman's Three Afterlife "Appearances". 274
      Losing Mom. 278
      Moving On 281

APPENDIX 285

Acknowledgements

On behalf of myself and my dearly departed brother and best friend, Norman, I would like to express my deepest appreciation for all those who contributed to our lives and careers. Although many names are listed in these pages, they make up only a small part of the "village" that nurtured us.

To my early friends (who later became our travel buddies) Vincent Scott and Thomas Copeland from St. Catherine of Siena Elementary School in Queens, New York.

To the many students at Christ the King High School.

To our bowling buddies, including Reggie Greene, Kim Long and Joann Marshall, to name only a few of those who were our support crew for bowling and a great many other activities and adventures.

To our St. John's University friends and classmates, including Clifton Diaz Stanley, Eric Reape, Cathy Shuemate and the very supportive Black student class of 1969.

To The Best of Friends (TBOF), headed by Tony Cooper, who invited us to manage Othello (their second nightclub in midtown Manhattan) after seeing our success in the college market—thus launching our nightclub career.

To Steve Roberts, who shared with us his banking knowledge and who became a spokesperson for The Dow family.

To our mentor in the late 1960s, Bob Cagle, a premier promoter of special events at the most exclusive venues.

To our staff at Othello/Justine's nightclub, including Justice Vasquez (who rose from coatroom attendant to Assistant Manager due to her amazing administrative and people skills), Robert Gaines, Marilyn Hubbard, Debbie Mitchell, Gloria Stevens, Dawne Steward, Lester and Dave Hill, Batman, Santi Ortiz, Jimmy Bryant, Jose Dozier, Jeff Brooks and Junior Nelson, just to name a few.

To the DJ's responsible for keeping the crowd motivated: Derrick Gaines, Richard Hot, Reggie Wells and thirty-plus years with Tommie Allen.

To Scotty "Flash" Bryant and Herman M., who put "Tuesday Nights at Justine's" on the map with their Uptown "flava."

To the friends of Justine's who supported our sensational Salsa Fridays with its live entertainment until its final days.

To my WWRL 1600 radio family of twenty years, including Adriane Gaines (who took me in after my office building was sold in 1998), Sid Small, Chesley Maddox-Dorsey, Anthony Small, Tony Morris, T. Robinson, Mike Hill, John C., Shevette Watson and many others.

ACKNOWLEDGEMENTS

To novelist Faye Thompson and Harlem's own Lana Turner for their continual encouragement to achieve the dream of this memoir.

To the many friends, patrons, and sponsors who supported us for nearly fifty years: Thank you, again and again!

To those who didn't make it to this moment, may you rest in heavenly bliss: Tommy Allen, Jose Dozier, Charlie Davis, Tony "Bird" Jenkins, Earl Samples, "Lori" Boykin, Robert Gaines, Eddie Bates, Jerry Boyce, Thomas Copeland Jr., Mel Doby, Giselle Jones, Alix DeJean, Andrea Barker, Frances White, Marcy Williams, Marty Strickland, Howard Lundy, Willie Dee, James Kornegay, Harold Maynard, Bucky Wynn, Barbara B. Smith, Charles "CP" Perry, Andre Harrell, Dr. Calvin Butts, Lee Robinson, Marlon Saunders, Jerry Pinks, Johnny 'The Duke' Allen and countless more.

One of my closest friends, Morris Rogers, passed away while I was completing this memoir, and I'd like to especially acknowledge him. Morris was an informative, non-judgmental, encouraging, entrepreneurial, funny and loyal good friend for over five decades. Morris was my confidante, and that was very helpful during the time after Justine's closed when I was grappling with where I was going to set up shop next.

He and I shared business and social similarities, too. Like me, he was a print broker, novice skier and tennis player. We especially bonded over tennis. In fact, after going to St. Louis for his wedding, I thought his then-fiancée Evelyn was going to kill us, since we'd played tennis the morning of their wedding. Even funnier was what happened afterward: we went to breakfast, and the waitress accidentally dropped our tray of food. Magically, Morris caught his own plate before it dropped, while the rest of us stared glumly at our food on the floor.

I babysat his miniature apartment in Fort Lee, New Jersey for a while when he was dating his beloved Evelyn, who lived in Harmon Cove in Secaucus. He didn't want to give up his apartment until he was sure about their marriage. The apartment-sitting also allowed me to crash in Fort Lee instead of driving all the way back home to my neighborhood near JFK airport.

Morris always thought he had the answers to many of my "situations," whether they were decisions about event sites or concerns about girlfriends. In 2005, he just knew he had found the woman of my dreams, but fate interfered. A week after he introduced me to this dream girl, I lost my brother Norman. It was a couple a months before I was able to connect with her, and we have since remained good friends.

What I admired about Morris was that he was never fearful of change; he went from one business to another. He left New Jersey to go to Pebble Beach, California to open a radio station with his wife and business partner. The Pebble Beach golf course was a big bonus—he could play golf there and boast about it to his buddies back on the East coast. Years later, he relocated to Florida to open an insurance business. Needless to say, I'll miss his friendship, laughter, his forever loyalty and his dedication to improving my life and social status. *Rest in Heaven, Morris, with Norman and Mom, who always loved you.*

ACKNOWLEDGEMENTS

I would also like to thank Lisa Farrington, who collaborated with me on this memoir. My first attempt to chronicle the lives of myself and my brother began in 2014, but creative differences between me and my then-coauthor caused the project to collapse. In 2019, the COVID pandemic further stalled the book's progress. Although disappointed, I never gave up, and in 2022, I at last returned to the project. That year, I was thrilled when Connie Delaigle, a friend and supporter throughout the decades, informed me that her sister, Lisa Farrington (another lifelong supporter and author in her own right) might be interested in assisting me in telling this story. Lisa was an ideal choice, since she had lived our history with us and attended our parties since the 1970s. It is important that the book reflects the real experiences and attitudes of the folks like Connie and Lisa, who took part in our events, and that their stories be told as part of the web of this long and far-reaching history.

Foreword

This memoir is the untold story of The Dow Twins—event specialists and entrepreneurs—who dominated the Black nightclub scene in New York City and beyond for half a century.

Imagine: identical twins born in New York City in the early 1950s to a working-class Black family. They were Evelyn and Reggie Dow's first-born sons—Norman and Harold. The unusual pair of adorable, chubby boys received a lot of attention growing up. They were well-loved by their parents, extended family, and family friends—all of whom doted on them. Physically, they were so much alike that even their own parents occasionally confused them with each other. But their personalities were quite different. One twin was reserved and serious; the other was outgoing and gregarious. They were an ideal team, complementing each other as they did.

> The Twins were not the same. There was a huge difference between them. Norman just wanted to have fun! Harold was the businessman and more reserved.
>
>
>
> Justice Vasquez
> Friend and collaborator for forty-five years

By the end of the 1960s, after a very happy and relatively carefree childhood, The Twins had found their way to St. John's University, where they began to grow a fan-base of followers who were drawn to their well-bred, smart, witty, charming and gallant personalities—a perfect formula for popularity. As cash-strapped students, the brothers decided to throw a pay party to raise money for a coveted stereo system: a humble goal that launched their laudatory and legendary careers as event hosts and party planners.

Their first professional event was held in the Black neighborhood of Jamaica, Queens, near where they grew up. For this initial venture, the young men hosted hundreds of friends and acquaintances who had found their way onto what would eventually become one of the most exclusive mailing lists in New York nightlife history.

That first party was a rousing success—a night of laughter and dancing without incident (miraculous, given the local presence of gangs and drugs in the area at that time). All the partygoers went home smiling and hoping for another event just like it. With no business experience but lots of street smarts, personality, marketing and financial acumen, by 1971 the two had found their calling as successful party producers. This was because, whatever else they may or may not have known at the tender age of nineteen, they knew how to throw a party. They had also grown six inches since high school and shed their baby fat to become attractive, enigmatic, and dynamic young men who operated first in Queens and then as nightclub managers in Midtown Manhattan, where few, if any, Black clubs were welcome at the time.

Their Queens patrons followed The Twins to Manhattan, while more from all five boroughs joined their clique. Their Manhattan venues were so popular, trend-setting, and sophisticated that they attracted an endless parade of celebrity clientele. Among the hundreds were iconic actress Elizabeth Taylor, comedian Eddie Murphy, pop artist Andy Warhol, Dallas Cowboys' Ed "Too Tall" Jones, world heavyweight boxing champion Joe Frazier, Dapper Dan, *Chic* disco band leader Nile Rodgers, basketball Hall of Famer Connie Hawkins, grammy powerhouses Stevie Wonder, *Labelle*, and the New York Knicks basketball team.

The two men known to all as "The Dow Twins" became preeminent New York City social influencers during the 1970s, '80s, '90s and beyond—and their path to success reads like a fairytale (except that it wasn't). It is a true story that speaks to their generous spirit, their fine minds, their business acumen, and their devotion to excellence in all that they did.

Fifty years of "social engineering" by the savvy management team of Harold and Norman Dow brought hundreds of thousands of Black folks happily together at some of the most celebrated "meet and greet" social venues in New York, as well as other major cities. They accomplished this with a self-engineered and exclusive patron list that reached masses of clients: at first via snail mail, and later, with the advent of the internet, electronically within minutes. The Dow Twins' epic journey as nightclub and social event moguls cannot be measured in ordinary terms. Their unprecedented success and longevity—half a century!— in the highly-competitive nightclub field was propelled by their indisputable strengths, which included resilience and the ability to establish and meet high standards, set goals, overcome obstacles, and face challenges with clear focus and cool heads.

The Dow Twins drew their impressive network of followers from some of the most active, appealing, exciting, and successful Black and LatinX professionals in New York and beyond. At a time (particularly the 1970s) when stereotypes of minorities were rampant, a significant number of upscale professionals of color found themselves chronically underserved in the upscale party market. The Dow Twins saw this need and filled it. Over time, their circle expanded to include a global coterie of cosmopolitan clientele who remained faithful to The Twins decade after decade—partying with them by the thousands quite literally from youth to old age.

Born in Queens, New York, Harold and Norman began their long career as event specialists while still in college. In 1973, they earned their Bachelor of Science degrees in Computer Science and Business Management from St. John's University, becoming the first in the Dow family to graduate from any university. They established themselves as a shrewd management team in the 1970s by orchestrating social events at celebrated New York City nightspots such as Manhattan's own Othello and Leviticus.

By 1979, Othello had transformed into the legendary Justine's, which became The Twins' home base and flagship venue for eight years during the Golden Age of Black nightlife in the tri-state area. More than a dance club, Justine's was a professional networking hub—a place to socialize, dance and meet new friends, as well as business associates. Among the other venues where the two established footholds and orchestrated events were the city's most celebrated dance clubs: Studio 54, The Palladium, The Red Parrot, the historic South Street Seaport, Waldorf-Astoria Hotel (where The Twins held their 20th Anniversary Black Tie Gala for a crowd of 800 people), Penn Station's Iron Horse, and the Old and New Copacabana venues, which attracted an international crowd.

After the age of the massive, multi-leveled New York City dance club ended and its archetypal venues closed their doors, The Dow Twins brought these places back to life each spring by treating their clientele to a "Justine's / Leviticus / Red Parrot" reunion that featured the sounds of the 1970s and '80s that had made those nightspots famous. They also held an "Annual Black on Black MASKquerade Gala" each year, celebrating in an atmosphere of fun, enchantment, and mystery with all-black attire and elegant, colorful masks.

In addition to these considerable projects, in 1986 The Twins established their own Manhattan Proper Café restaurant and bar in their old neighborhood—making it one of the only upscale social venues in the area. Featuring jazz and comedy nights, renowned DJs, and multiple annual special events, The Proper (as it later became known) served the public faithfully for over three decades from 1986 until 2017.

Perhaps the most acclaimed and broadly-attended events produced by The Twins were their annual fêtes aboard the USS Intrepid Air, Sea and Space Museum—an actual aircraft carrier docked on the Hudson River in New York City. Each year, for over twenty-five consecutive years from 1985 to 2010, attendance at The Twins' annual soirées surpassed record attendance from the previous year. Consistently meeting standards of quality, elegance, atmosphere, and turnout, this ongoing undertaking established a track record that opened The Twins' events up to major corporate sponsors. Each year, the Intrepid event became more high-profile, and sponsorship increased correspondingly. As a result of this infusion of corporate funding, The Twins were able to keep the price of admission reasonable for their ever-devoted clientele (similar events organized by other promoters cost significantly more). Among their sponsorship innovations was the establishment of a popular new beverage—the *Alizé* product brand—for Kobrand Corporation Wines and Spirits, which became one of The Twins' most loyal sponsors.

Ever aware of the impending challenges they faced in sustaining a captive audience after nearly twenty years of local success, in the late 1980s The Twins developed an avant-garde twentieth-century business model. Rethinking the notion of specializing only in a regional market, they understood that their future professional longevity could only be maintained if they shifted focus to a national and even international market. From 1991 to 2007, The Twins partnered with The National Brotherhood of Skiers (NBS) to enhance the organization's celebrated ski summits in Vail and Steamboat, Colorado, Park City, Utah and many other acclaimed sites in Eastern and Western Canada. The Twins added exclusive networking opportunities and events to the customary NBS convention fare, vastly improving engagement and attendance.

Reinventing themselves and their business approach as needed, The Dow Twins demonstrated the skills, agility, management acumen and expertise necessary to access new markets, while maintaining the dedication and commitment of existing ones. They were visionaries, to say the least, with a track record for taking special events to new levels of entertainment and efficacy that left audiences yearning for more.

The Dow Twins did more than succeed in business. Ever mindful of their commitment to give back to the community, they used their influence to help to organize fundraising events for many worthy causes, to which they themselves also contributed. They consulted for the New York Urban League, The United Negro College Fund, The Dave Winfield Foundation, The Negro Ensemble Company, Pathways for Youth, The Dance Theatre of Harlem, The USS Intrepid Foundation, the South Africa Mandela Project, the Hurricane Katrina Relief Fund, and the St. John's University Alumni Association. They also donated their expertise and funds to benefit The Jackie Robinson's Foundation for a decade from 1991 to 2001; and eventually founded the Reginald N. Dow Memorial Scholarship in memory of their

FOREWORD

father, raising $50,000 to support high school graduating seniors in their college endeavors.

When Harold's beloved brother Norman passed away in his sleep on November 10th, 2005, breaking the hearts of hundreds of thousands of friends and followers from around the world, the Norman F. Dow Foundation was launched and its inaugural fundraiser held aboard the USS Intrepid on Saturday, December 6th, 2008. Harold further honored his brother's memory in 2011 when he organized a second benefit on October 15th, 2011, at the home of the New York Mets (and Norman's favorite) baseball team: CitiField. A third event—Norman's 10th Anniversary Memorial Gala—was held on October 10th, 2015, at the famed Terrace on the Park at the old World's Fair grounds in Queens (where *Men in Black* was filmed).

Harold lamented not being able to host their next landmark gathering: "It was disappointing that we had to forego our 50th Anniversary Celebration at Terrace on the Park, planned for 2021, due to the devastating pandemic that rocked our communities and the world." Subsequent to the pandemic and after a lifetime of professional and personal achievement, Harold retired to his beloved childhood neighborhood in 2022.

The memoir to follow details the rollercoaster ride taken by The Dow Twins in their shared journey, and it recounts the many fascinating, funny, and sometimes sad stories that marked their lives and the lives of those who were fortunate enough to know them. As one of those fortunate people, I can only hope that at least one last party is in the cards (even we're all there in wheelchairs and walkers) and, if not, that we'll all meet again on a Dow Twins' dancefloor in the hereafter.

Lisa Farrington

CANCELED due to the 2019 – 2021 pandemic

Introduction

Allow me to introduce myself. I am Harold A. Dow, who, along with my brother, Norman F. Dow, made up The Dow Twins. In 2005, when my twin brother passed away, I knew I had to record our story...

My brother and I formed an urban marketing company in the early 1970s to provide venues, themes, and activities for upwardly mobile college students and friends. Nearly half a century later, well into the new millennium, we were still catering to our loyal followers, who had all grown up and were still looking to enjoy New York's nightlife in a secure and convivial environment. What began as a few hundred patrons had grown exponentially over time, eventually numbering, quite literally, in the tens of thousands. Of these, many had been attending our events faithfully for decades.

In the 1970s, '80s and '90s, Norman and I were known as social influencers long before the term was coined. We started as college students at St. John's University (SJU) as the disco craze was exploding. Our modest goal at the time was to secure a three-part stereo system, so we hosted our first event at Rochdale Village auditorium, near our home. The turnout was amazing, and the die was cast in 1971. We decided then that this was going to be our business.

We started thinking about the idea of bringing our friends from different colleges together to capitalize on the exploding dance scene. During our second year at SJU, we began hosting parties on and off campus and continued to do so until we graduated in 1973.

Anyone who remembers us from those years will recall the identical twins who were always together and drove an orange Volkswagen Fastback. Or they might remember our classmate Cliff Diaz, who was tall, dark, and handsome and who (not surprisingly) received numerous invitations from the ladies to attend their birthday parties. As a result, the three of us had a very lively party schedule.

After graduation, my brother and I realized that commuting students on various campuses had no place to go during school holidays and breaks when campuses were closed. So, we decided to organize a few special events at different locations around the city that would be convenient to tri-state area university students. By this time, we had met The Best of Friends (TBOF), a group of young entrepreneurs comprised of eight young Black men mostly from the New York City area. Like Norman and I, TBOF loved to bowl, and we indulged in this pastime often, which created a real bond between us.

Meeting TBOF in those early years greatly fostered our future success because they were among the first successful Black discotheque owners in Manhattan. At that time their nightclub, Leviticus, was *the* place to be for the mature adult crowd. By 1975, TBOF was looking for a team that could successfully handle their second nightclub, Othello, located on Eighth Avenue.

TBOF offered Norman and I an opportunity to manage their club and to develop it into a social networking and dancing venue for Black college students. With no experience or concrete

INTRODUCTION

business plan, we left Queens and headed to Manhattan. We promoted Othello feverishly, distributing thousands of homemade flyers to partygoers standing in line on the sidewalks of Manhattan while waiting to be admitted to one of the city's many discos.

Othello (later Justine's) quickly became *the* place to go for a younger, college-aged audience. Thanks to TBOF, my brother and I were given the opportunity to create, run, and grow our own business and brand. We filled a need not previously met in New York City—to provide elegant, upmarket Midtown party venues of Soul and Latin music for young urbanites who, during these years, had few other choices.

We settled on a nightclub formula that involved DJs who played the energizing up-tempo disco music being heard on the radio at the time. We also put in the "legwork" required to secure names and addresses for our ever-growing database. We were intent on only reaching out to a special kind of upscale consumer and to those whom we had met personally. This allowed us to create a specific type of party environment. We couldn't afford to finance radio spots in the early years, so we did the next best thing—we hung out. We attended all types of activities and functions and met as many folks as possible. We made friends and invited them to our events. They invited their friends, and so on, and so on. Ladies were ideal additions to our event list, since they always traveled in groups (whereas guys tended to come alone). To engage the ladies, we planned large-scale themed events such as Sadie Hawkins Nights, Waistline Parties, Flight Attendant Nights, Salsa Friday's Latin Nights, Astrological Sign Birthday parties (including our own Gemini / Cancer celebrations), and our annual MASKquerade gala.

Our greatest accomplishments were three-fold: securing the aircraft carrier, the USS Intrepid, as one of the most unique event venues in New York (if not the country); secondly, convincing independent promoters and influencers to join us, thus greatly expanding our efforts; and thirdly, successfully negotiating with major sponsors, who readily agreed to underwrite our events due to our impeccable reputation as successful event hosts and businessmen. We established a track record of success so that we could approach sponsors of any level and assure them that we had the capacity and sway to market their products to our patrons.

Our sponsors ranged from beverage and insurance companies to car manufacturers and travel agencies. Their support subsidized the costs of catering and, on occasion, spirit prices so that we could keep our admission fees low—which made our events affordable for our guests and, as a result, grew our business. Norman and I understood that one hit wonders were a dime a dozen; and that we first had to bet on ourselves before we could convince others to believe in what we were selling. We counted very much on *ourselves*.

In the pre-sponsorship years, we gambled on ourselves many times. We wagered that folks would come to our first-ever event held at Rochdale Village in Queens; and that they would keep coming when we moved our focus to Midtown Manhattan venues such as Othello or the Circle Line cruises; and again to upstate New York for ski outings, to the Grand Ballroom of The Waldorf Astoria Hotel (for our record-breaking 20th Anniversary Black Tie Gala); and to many more events too numerous to name. We were very fortunate. Our diligence, hard work, and seemingly uncanny ability to be in the right place at the right time helped us to launch and maintain a phenomenally successful business from 1971 to 2021. Not bad for the once-chubby little twins from Queens.

INTRODUCTION

My brother and I also shared a social commitment to "give back" to the community. This effort manifested in successful fundraising efforts for the numerous non-profit organizations mentioned in the Foreword, including the Jackie Robinson Fund, the Negro Ensemble Company, and the Arthur Ashe Foundation, among many others. Having benefitted from university education ourselves, we were especially interested in supporting the educational endeavors of financially disadvantaged youths. We accomplished this through our annual scholarship program.

I began the journey of chronicling our history as The Dow Twins several years ago, and it is with joy and nostalgia that I share these memories with you. After my brother passed, it became critical for me to record and remember our lives. But this memoir is not only about us; it is also about our peers—Black folks like us who were born in the 1950s and were often among the first in their families to attend college and to become successful entrepreneurs, doctors, lawyers and professionals in many fields. These high achievers became our loyal followers. Their hearts and souls are rooted in the Black community. They worked hard and, like us, they partied hard. Their stories are here, too.

Harold A. Dow

CHAPTER ONE

How It All Began

1950s Hit Songs

"Tears on My Pillow" by Little Anthony & The Imperials
"Why Do Fools Fall in Love" by Frankie Lymon & The Teenagers

June 20th, 1951

>Wow—Mom over the moon.

>What a shock—twins.

>Norman and Harold born. Big surprise, since we were expecting only one child.

>In those days no x-rays or sonograms were taken—it might have been bad for the baby.

I was on a thousand-calorie diet because I was gaining weight too fast, not realizing I was carrying twins. And they were facing one another, so only the heartbeat of the child in front was heard. At birth two children appeared, weighing 5 lb 08 oz and 5 lb 10 oz. Born healthy.

They walked early but didn't talk early. We took them to all kinds of specialists to see why they didn't talk. At that time, the only explanation doctors could give us was that they had their own language and that they understood each other; and since we, as parents, anticipated their every need, it wasn't necessary for them to talk.

Well maybe they were right, because once Norman started talking, he never stopped; and he never stopped smiling, either.

We exposed them to music, dragging them to the children's musical programs at Queens College until they said they'd had enough (Bernstein classical on Saturday mornings—teaching the children the difference between various instruments and sounds).

Music was my thing! For them, sports were next on the agenda…

There was football, baseball, and bowling. I was glad they ruled out football—so I didn't have to go to the games to watch them get mauled. Baseball had looked like it was going to be next, since they both seemed destined to be catchers, like Roy Campanella.

In the end, bowling won out. They both liked it and did well. They almost won a bowling scholarship. I didn't have to buy a single turkey during the holidays because they were always in what they called the "Turkey Roll" tournament and would win a turkey. They were in a "Father and Son" league when their father died. Since the bowling season wasn't done, two of their father's friends took over and finished out the season with them. Their father was well-liked and a generous person. Norman was named for our mother's side of the family and Harold was named for Reggie's side of family.

I tried to expose the fellows to everything; we didn't leave out swimming. That was a real challenge. There were swimming meets, practice meets and more. Then we had to campaign for them to wear matching swimming trunks, since all the fellows on the team wore trunks of different styles and colors. It became my job to get matching trunks for the team. What a task!

Mrs. Evelyn Dow

My grandma Frances Sims, parents Evelyn S. & Reginald N. Dow, and grandpa Arthur Dow

Childhood

When Norman and I were toddlers in the early 1950s, twins were rare that, so we received a lot of attention. As youngsters, we were always together. Mom tried to dress us alike but that got old fast, and we started dressing ourselves in different styles.

Growing up, we never really had many arguments; and if you were a friend of one of us, you were a friend of both of us. We were competitive in sports like swimming and bowling but always in a congenial way, accepting that one or the other was better.

We learned how to treat each other and those around us by watching the example of our parents (especially our mom), our grandma Frances and our Aunt Vivian. Our grandmother took us to school every day, providing us with sage advice along the way. Our father was a popular MTA bus driver and interesting to his coworkers because he was a young Black man raising twin boys. He taught us how to swim at Jones Beach. Being around positive role models and having various sports outlets definitely kept us on the right track and focused on "doing the right thing" in life.

We were raised Catholic and attended grammar at St. Catherine of Sienna, where the nuns put the fear of God in us and kept us on the straight and narrow. Outside of school, we spent a lot of our time in the St. Albans Bowling Alley. We could be found there every week, hanging out with friends and their parents. Ideally for us, the alley was only minutes from their house. The Q4 bus took us to the Long Island Railroad station near the bowling alley, and we could walk the rest of the way in minutes.

Norman made the All-City Championship Team as a youth, which took him Upstate to compete for the State Championship title in his division. Our friends were players in the league (Kim

HOW IT ALL BEGAN

Long, Joann Marshall and Reggie Truly Greene) who pushed us to be our most competitive; they even defeated us on occasion. Most of the league members came from bowling families who also encouraged us. Bowling was, we realized, a safe outlet for our youthful energy during the 1960s.

I met Harold and Norman in the first grade at St. Catherine of Sienna grammar school. There was Norman and Harold, Thomas Copeland, the Gittens sisters, and me. We all met in 1960 – 1961. St Catherine's did not have any extracurricular activities, so we had few social outlets other than house parties. Norman and Harold were one of only two sets of twins in our circle, which gave them a social status beyond our own. Everyone knew of The Dow Twins. By the eighth grade, Norman and Harold started to use their popularity at parties. I'm not sure when they really turned it into business, but I do know that the seed was planted by the time they were in high school.

Besides going to parties, Norman, Harold and I spent a good amount of time during our younger years at the Copeland home. Thomas' mother didn't work, unlike Mrs. Dow and my mother, so she was always there to supervise. It was a great hangout. We played card games like Bid Whist and board games like Monopoly. It really was a great childhood, in retrospect. Thomas' sister, Samantha (Sam), and his brother, Kenneth, were close to our age, so they usually joined us for the fun and games.

Vincent Scott
Lifelong friend

Harold and Norman dressed to attend the Key Women cotillion

Norman, Mom, Dad and Harold with our dog, Pal

HOW IT ALL BEGAN

I grew up in New Jersey, but several of my aunts lived in Queens. My Aunt Helen's house was next door to a family with twin sons: Harold and Norman. Because they were only a year older than me, my family was determined that we should be friends. Whenever I attended the mandatory family gatherings, they connected me with the little boys next door. I saw them as two smart, geeky, chubby guys who were always smiling and, frankly, got on my nerves. Of course, at eight or nine years old, who wanted to deal with boys at all? As we became teenagers, we became more friendly and hung out together when I visited my family. But again: smart, geeky, chubby, smiley ... nice, but corny! My family secretly thought that one of them—either of them—would be great husband material and consistently forced me to hang out with them ... I say this with my eyes rolling, as they did then (smile).

꽃

Barbara Cheives
Lifelong friend

As tweens, Norman and I felt we'd had enough of parochial school, and we wanted to attend Andrew Jackson High School, where so many of our friends went. Instead, our mother sent us to the gender-segregated Catholic high school, Christ the King, to keep us on the right path, which it did. During these years, we became fast friends with Vinny Scott, Thomas Copeland, and Anna Perez (who went on to work for the first Mrs. George Bush in The White House). As a group, we socialized often, especially on summer weekends. We and our families made trips to

Jones Beach to body surf the massive waves. Towards the end of each summer season, before school began, we would go to Bear Mountain with more friends from our block in Jamaica, including Garth Ramsey and George Latimer's family.

Upon graduation from Christ the King, Norman and Harold began their career giving parties. Norman used his personality and charm to promote the events while Harold would handle the advertisement. Thomas and I would be the wing men and do the grunt work (smile) for every party. Even though we had all gone to different high schools—Norman and Harold to Christ the King; Thomas to Brooklyn Prep; and I to St. Francis Prep—we remained good friends.

This was because of bowling. My dad ran a teen bowling league on Saturday morning. So, every weekend Norman, Harold, Thomas and I went bowling. Norman was a natural left-hander, while Harold bowled with his right hand. This was probably one of the only things that were different between The Twins. Harold was a better bowler with a higher average, but Norman held his own.

Bowling became an important part of all our lives. Norman and Harold joined their high school bowling league and the Jr. Gothamites, which was a competitive traveling teen bowling team. We traveled throughout the city, challenging other teen bowling teams. It was the Saturday Jr. bowling league and the Gothamites that brought Kim Long to the group—and she became Norman's first girlfriend.

HOW IT ALL BEGAN

When they were about sixteen years old, The Twins lost their grandfather, Arthur Dow, their father, Reginald Dow, and their grandmother, Mrs. Frances Sims. After this triple tragedy, it was just Mrs. Dow and The Twins, since Mr. Dow was adopted and Mrs. Dow was an only child. Thomas and I and all their friends were as supportive as we could be. Mrs. Dow did everything to make sure that her boys had whatever they needed.

Vincent Scott
Lifelong friend

The Crew: Harold, Thomas, Vinny and Norman

On April 20th, 1968, when we were in high school, our father died. We were sixteen years old. It was a day of reckoning. It was the first truly dark moment in our family's otherwise gratifying history. Our father, Reginald Dow, was a hardworking, patient and loving man. He was a pillar of strength in our home, and he left a legacy of warmth and fond memories, even though he was only in our lives for sixteen years.

Reggie, as his friends called him, was always there for the important moments. He taught Norman and I how to be good men through his own acts of kindness and by teaching us how to swim, ride bikes, and listen to what our grandma and mom had to say. Since he worked for the MTA, he made sure the other bus drivers watched over us whenever we were in the street. They reported to Reggie when they saw us riding around Queens during his days at work.

One day, dad gladly accepted a gifted dog named Pal into our lives. Ironically, Pal protected and comforted us in the days following April 20th. Our "Harlem" grandfather, Arthur Dow (who had adopted our father as a child) molded dad into the popular gentleman and World War II veteran that he became. Our live-in grandmother, Frances, had raised our mother in the same way: to be a beautiful person and loving mom. Grandma Frances also co-parented us. She would take us to grammar school, and she would stop at the local candy store and "sweeten us up," even when we misbehaved. Ours truly was a happy and carefree existence until that fateful day in 1968.

The ordeal of our father's death began just two short weeks after the assassination of Dr. Martin Luther King Jr., which had already cast a shadow over our home. Dad was rushed to Jamaica Hospital with inexplicable abdominal pain. He had always been strong and healthy; his sudden physical weakness caused our family much concern. The diagnosis was appendicitis, but his temperature was so high that the doctors could not operate immediately.

At the same time, our Harlem grandfather (who had aged significantly since the passing of his wife) was also in failing health and was in Harlem Hospital in grave condition. Our father was not immediately alerted to grandfather's illness, so as not to add to aggravate his condition. A few days later, Grandma Frances also took sick. Faced with this triple crisis, our mom did all she could to steady herself and her sons with the help of her best friend Vivian. Between the two, they coped with the three sick family members.

The following Saturday morning, Norman and I were downstairs in our home when the phone rang. I answered and could hear my mother pick up the extension upstairs. A voice on the phone said that "Mr. Dow" had passed away. At first, we weren't sure which Mr. Dow the doctor was referring to. It was my dad. I remember that my mother screamed, "Oh no!"

We had almost no time to process this tremendous loss because a few short hours later, much to our horror, Grandma Frances also passed away. The weight of this tragedy was crushing, especially for mom, who had lost her mother and husband (who was also her best friend) only hours apart. Norman and I witnessed with awe as mom handled all of this with grace and humility. She stayed strong for us; and she had the strength and fortitude to bury three family members that year (my grandfather died a few months later) while facing an uncertain future, especially with her sons soon leaving her to head off to college.

Norman and I had originally planned to enroll at Howard University in Washington, D.C. Given the circumstances, however, we decided that we could not abandon our mother at this crucial time. We chose, instead, to remain at home and attend St. John's University.

During the difficult days and months following our family's misfortune, we felt blessed to have the support of the many friends of our parents, who stepped up and filled in some of the voids created by our losses. Even though we had our father for only sixteen years, he remained in our hearts for the rest of our lives; and his memory got our mom through some tough years. Ironically, the idea of creating an event planning business was the silver lining, since we now wanted to become earners to support our mother as much as possible, and to include her in our projects. This opportunity would present itself only a year or so later, with our first party.

As our careers at Christ the King High School (known affectionately then as the "Graveyard" since it was surrounded by cemeteries) came to a close, the time had come for us to slim down. Norman and I were tired of being referred to as the "Pillsbury Dough Boys" in school and in the neighborhood. So, we made the decision to reduce our food intake by eating nothing but salads and low-calorie meals. Tennis was the main exercise vehicle for our weight loss. Norman took it one step further by wearing a plastic sweat outfit. Without any medical advice we nearly starved, and we only survived our diet regimen that summer of 1969 by sheer will.

Another concern for us that summer was getting a car. In the outer boroughs of New York City, you didn't even consider turning sixteen without getting a drivers' permit, and Norman and I were no exception. We had already learned to drive with the help of our dad; and once we passed the driver's test, we couldn't wait to get our licenses and buy a car.

The opportunity came one very dry summer season before entering college. We were fortunate to land summer jobs at the Jamaica Water Company, which needed extra help to monitor water usage during the drought. Our duties included driving around the neighborhood in small pick-up trucks checking on residential sprinkler use. The only problem was that we didn't know how to drive a stick shift. The staff at the Water Company must have really liked us because they taught us the necessary skills using company vehicles on company grounds in only two days (and with maybe one stripped gear).

We were hanging out that summer with our friend Michael Levy, his cousin Marsha, and her girlfriend Debbie (who Norman was dating at the time). On our lunch breaks, we would all meet at our house in Ashleigh Park near Linden and Merrick Boulevards to play pool in the basement.

By the end of that summer of 1969, Norman and I had had each lost thirty pounds, grown several inches, and earned $3,000—enough to buy our first car, an orange Volkswagen Fastback. We were now ready for the St. John's University experience...

Joellen & sister Alexis G. leaning on our infamous Orange VW Fastback

Surviving St. John's

St. John's was a good fit for The Twins, and their promoting skills flourished.

❦

Vincent Scott
Lifelong friend

Much like our experience at St. Catherine's and Christ the King, when Norman and I entered St. John's University in 1969 as freshmen, there were very few people of color. However, unlike high school, where there were only half-a-dozen Black kids, in college the people of color numbered nearly seventy, or slightly less than 1% of the 8,000 students on campus. It was the largest Black class to enter St. John's University (SJU) up to that point.

Having dozens of Black classmates was a major difference for us. Norman and I naturally gravitated towards people who looked like us. In fact, the Black students in general gravitated towards each other; and the folks we met that first semester became our longtime friends.

The White students were friendly to us, but even though we did share some activities with them (like bowling), these interactions were limited, and Whites and Blacks mostly went their separate ways. Nevertheless, Norman and I always saw our White classmates as equals—no better or worse, no more or less ignorant, or intelligent—just people we went to school with. In fact, our exposure to White kids throughout our educational careers had a positive effect on our business lives after college—Norman and I never had a problem communicating or negotiating with the many White club owners, sponsors, and managers we met. We were as at ease with Whites as we were with Blacks, and we were able to secure contracts for upscale facilities that were normally unavailable to Black clientele.

In fact, we grew up in an integrated neighborhood. In the 1950s and early 1960s, the communities of Jamaica and St. Albans in southeast Queens were home to many Whites who had yet to move away to Nassau and Suffolk counties on Long Island in their efforts to put distance between themselves and the incoming African Americans.

While we got along well with White kids in the classroom, that was not always the case outside of school. We sometimes experienced racial tension if we biked or walked through the neighborhoods of Springfield Gardens, Laurelton, or Ozone Park, which were still mainly White at the time. When we found ourselves in these areas, the older kids would harass us, cursing at us or trying to take our bikes. Their goal was to run us out of their so-called "all-White" neighborhoods (although by the mid-1960s, as more and more Blacks moved into these areas, the Whites left *en masse*.)

I personally believe that their racist attitudes were inherited from their parents, and that if Norman and I had grown up in a segregated neighborhood it would have been a detriment to our future development in life and in business. Integration was key. I still believe that young people must learn to get along with all races in our global community because anyone—Black, White, or other—can be equally good or bad. You have to look past the surface.

Nevertheless, on campus at SJU, we and our Black classmates often congregated together, especially in Marillac Hall, which was campus hub for the Black student community. While hanging out in Marillac, we learned about all the Black events and activities happening on campus and beyond.

At mid-semester that first year, we also learned of a call around the nation to establish Black Studies curriculum on campuses. The Black upperclassmen at SJU immediately heeded this call and requested the participation of freshman and sophomores. Most of us, including Norman and I, were hesitant to join the campaign, mainly because we were new to the university and wary of the consequences to our scholarships and status if we participated in any kind of protest; but when a demonstration was launched, we joined despite our concerns.

Student protesters chose to march to the President's Tower office. As we descended upon it, we could see that the New York Police Department (NYPD) was ominously circling the campus, waiting to step in and quell any unrest. Seeing this, the upperclassmen wisely suggested that those on scholarships "step off" so as not to jeopardize their financial support. Thankfully, their proposal turned out to be unnecessary because the university's progressive President, Reverend Joseph T. Cahill, agreed to establish a Black Studies program and made it clear to the NYPD that their services were not needed. Bravo St. John's and Father Cahill!

The University's first Black Studies professor was Leslie Agard Jones (currently Dean of the College of Education at William Patterson University in Wayne, New Jersey). He had a huge influence on Norman and me. He was the first professor we'd ever met who looked like us. We could always go to him with our problems and concerns, and he would help to explain or resolve them. To us, he was the perfect addition to the faculty at SJU, and we remained in touch with him for many years.

In fact, later in our lives, Professor Jones encouraged my brother and me to invest $100,000 in the Brooklyn Union Gas Brownstone Rehab or "Cinderella" Project. Instead, in 1984, we purchased real estate in New Jersey, including a three-bedroom duplex condo in a gated community called Harmon Cove Townhouses, situated about twelve minutes from Justine's via the Lincoln Tunnel.

In addition to the founding of a Black Studies program and hiring Professor Jones, the student protests led to the formation of a chapter of Haraya (a national Pan African Student Coalition) on campus in 1969. It was truly an exciting time.

St. John's University 1969 Haraya Members

Another issue that came up during that first semester at SJU was the Selective Service Draft and the statistics associated with it. At that time, 25% of the American forces came from poor communities; 55% from working class families; and 20% from the middle class. Very few came from the upper class. African Americans were assigned to combat units in Vietnam at twice the rate of White soldiers; and in some units, they made up as much as 60% of the troops. At age eighteen, young men were required to register with the Selective Service. Norman and I had a high draft number, which meant that, despite our enrollment in college (which should have deferred us), we were very likely to be drafted into the Vietnam conflict.

The problem for the Armed Services was our father's recent passing the year before. The Selective Service program was not permitted to draft all the sons of a fatherless family, so they had to decide which of us should be drafted. Their decision took almost a year while the Vietnam conflict was ending. Thankfully, our Selective Service letter arrived after the draft policy had been suspended; we decided not to open it. We didn't want to know which one of us they'd chosen. Instead, we went on with our studies and quest to become entrepreneurs.

Little known to our friends is the fact that Norman and I inherited our entrepreneurial spirit from our mom, who was an event planner in her own right. She planned things for her "crew"—a group of mostly single women whom she knew before and after her marriage. She planned multiple trips for them, such as Dude Ranch weekends, Sag Harbor outings, and a trip to the then-Peg Leg Bates Country Club in Kerhonkson, New York (made up of a predominantly Black membership until its closing in 1989).

Just like her sons' parties, our mother's events included single friends and couples. On one memorable event in the early 1970s she and her sister-friend Vivian hosted a Mother's Day Brunch at Belmont Racetrack in Elmont, Long Island. The ladies arrived at the track dressed to the nines with designer spring dresses and fabulous hats. With buffet dining and gambling as the main courses, how could they go wrong? This became an annual event called "Les Amies," meaning "The Girlfriends."

In 1971, we held our first event—a Black Students College Party—in the auditorium of the co-op community of Rochdale Village in Jamaica, Queens. We were sophomores by this time—when the disco craze was exploding—and we wanted to provide entertainment for our fellow university students and friends in the tri-state area. Our initial goal was a modest one: to secure a three-part stereo system. Norman and I had the idea to bring friends from different universities together to capitalize on the exploding dance scene.

Our goal was achieved with the aid of a classmate, Cliff Stanley Diaz— "The Third Twin" (who would become a bus driver, Board Chairman and "face" of the Rochdale Village Co-op for seventeen years). Though shy, Cliff's tall, good looks earned him numerous invitations from female students to attend their parties; and he'd share these with me and Norman. In a single evening, we could drive to several parties where we'd charm not the ladies, but their parents, so they'd give their daughters permission to attend our events.

Parents loved us because we dressed well and behaved like gentlemen. We wore sport jackets and were always polite. By attending these parties (many of which were held in upscale Queens and Long Island neighborhoods such as St. Albans, Laurelton, Valley Stream, and Hempstead), we began to build a client base—a project that continued throughout our college years. Thanks to these efforts, the turnout at our first party was incredible.

Between our second year at SJU and graduation in 1973, we visited several more campuses up and down the northeast coast including Mt. Holyoke (Mass), Howard University (DC), Adelphi (Long Island), Hunter College (Manhattan), Farleigh Dickerson (NJ), Springfield College (Mass), Boston University (Mass), Queens College (NYC), City College (Manhattan), FIT (Fashion Institute of Technology in Manhattan), BMCC (Borough of Manhattan Community College), the University of Hartford (CT), Amhurst College (MA), and Sarah Lawrence College (Bronxville, NY). We even drove our VW Fastback to an event at the University of Tennessee.

Our graduation party was our capstone event. We knew that it would be crowded and noisy, so we warned our neighbors in advance; they were very agreeable and supportive. They brought desserts to our house and parked their cars in their driveways instead of on the street, to make room for our guests' cars. Mom and her friends prepared food, too. We fenced in the outdoor party space, including the double garage and driveway. As they say, the "PARTY WAS ON." Once the party really got going and the DJ was rocking the crowd, many arriving guests complained that they had to park four or five blocks away on the other side of Merrick Boulevard, because our guests' cars were parked everywhere else.

After a while, Norman and I noticed that folks we hadn't invited had started showing up. Apparently, they'd heard about our party at a barbeque that was being held at the home of Robert Gaines (a former Navy chef) on Sayres Avenue about a half a mile away; and they decided to crash our celebration. As the crowd grew, mom began to worry about what the neighbors would say but, as we'd hoped, there were no complaints, and our guests were very polite and respectful of mom's property. Thanks to the party-crashers, we got to meet the nearby barbecue host—Robert Gaines—who was known for his culinary skills. He became a friend and, later, the first chef at Manhattan Proper Café, which Norman and I opened in Queens in 1985.

Not surprisingly, this was the first and last party at Mrs. Dow's house. One overcrowded bash was enough for her. That said, she really did like our friends. In fact, there were very few people that Norman and I bought home whom mom didn't like.

During our college days, she loved catering to our friends (in smaller numbers, of course) and some of them became very close to her, keeping in touch for many years. Mom was generous with her time and advice to those who needed it—just as she was with me and Norman.

Many of the friends we brought home would enjoy long conversations with mom. She was genuinely interested in their lives and views, and she was never judgmental. That was the Gemini in her. In particular, our friends Vinny Scott, Thomas Copeland and another set of twins named Andrea and Annette Barker, were always at the house; sometimes, mom would invite them to Thanksgiving dinners, along with our Aunt Vivian.

> During this time, The Twins kept in touch with Thomas [Copeland] and me by taking road trips, visiting Thomas, who was in school in Washington DC, and me in Springfield, Mass. Norman and Harold were the first to own a car from our little group. It was not a standard, but an automatic orange Fastback Volkswagen. I loved that car. The Fastback had many tales, but the one that comes to my mind concerns our trip to visit one of Norman's girlfriends, who was attending school in Tennessee. We all were assigned a time to drive the fifteen-hour trip. I was unlucky enough to get the night shift. I ended up driving the car into a ditch and was called "ditchy" for the rest of the trip—and after.
>
> During their college years, tennis entered The Twins' lives through the Barker twins, Andrea and Annette. They were avid tennis players who played at Liberty Park (Harold still plays there today). They introduced tennis to all of us. Norman and Harold wanted to play not only

for the love of the game, but also for the exercise. They were always concerned about their weight and dieting, ever since high school.

After college, we went into our different fields of study. Harold and Norman graduated in Computer Science, Thomas went into banking, and I went on to teach science.

Vincent Scott
Lifelong friend

After graduation, Norman and I were offered entrée positions in computer systems at IBM in Tarrytown, New York. Hmmm. A desk job, or a life as entrepreneurs in the party business? I don't have to tell you which road we took. We decided to turn down the IBM opportunity and went into business for ourselves as party planners.

Mom was a little concerned that we were giving up an established career for what might very well be a temporary one. Since our dad's passing, however, mom had become a little more liberal, and she allowed us to make this choice ourselves. It also comforted her that this path would not require us to move away to Tarrytown. Instead, we would be able to continue working from home where we lived with her; and we could include her in the planning of some of our projects. Staying home also allowed us to save up money for the purchase of our own home down the road.

Another plus for mom was that, as long as we lived at home, she could see to it that we didn't have any overnight female guests. Mom was very clear on that matter. But, like many of the Baby Boomers of our circle, we were less interested in romantic entanglements than in finishing college or graduating school, getting good jobs and, of course, partying—going out dancing and mixing and mingling with friends at different venues around the city.

Our years at SJU had allowed us to spend more time around Black folks our own age for a change. It helped us to come into our own, to connect with our male peers, to overcome our childhood shyness, become at ease with women and to showcase our distinct personalities.

Prior to college, most of our socializing had been on the tennis court or in bowling alleys—not at school. In addition, our college experience connected us with Black students on different campuses, facilitated the launching of our careers in event planning, and so much more. We were able to create opportunities for our cohort to enjoy themselves while also making new friends across the five boroughs and beyond—something very few folks our age group were doing at the time. By graduation, not only had we visited a dozen different universities, but we had also promoted our events at nightclub locations all over New York. During these years we made decisions about the type of dress, music, patronage, and venues we preferred.

We assessed the nature of our clientele at the different college campuses; we surveyed various genres of music, downtown vs. uptown atmospheres, and where we should center our locations in NYC. While at SJU, we laid the groundwork for our futures as entrepreneurs.

A key relationship that came out of this period in our lives was with The Best of Friends (TBOF). They were a Black entertainment force in New York City, and they were keen to work with us, since we were rocking a totally different crowd from their adult professional one—*Black college students*. We came to understand that TBOF's interest in us made perfect sense—to reel in the next generation of party goers. We very much appreciated their confidence in us, which allowed us to learn more about the business such as club staffing and management.

Unlike TBOF, however, Norman and I were never that interested in ownership. Instead, we enjoyed going into different spaces and enhancing what the owner had already created. It allowed us to stay fresh; to build a theme around the already existing reputation and aura of a venue; and to present it to our folks as something new. Our main objective was to keep our events interesting enough for folks to return again and again, by creating new ideas while doubling down on the ones that were already successful. With college under our belts, we were ready for the big time.

Early invitations

HOW IT ALL BEGAN

Norman and Harold playing backgammon with actor Calvin Lockart at Leviticus

Modeling showcase at Othello

Another fun & creative promotional flyer to promote business in the lates 70s and 80s

CHAPTER TWO

Never Let Them See You Sweat

1970s Hit Songs

"War" by Edwin Starr
"Young, Gifted and Black" by Nina Simone
"How Do You Keep the Music Playing" by Tito Nieves

The Dow Twins' unique ideas of waistline, age, dance parties, and other successes caught the eye of an older, very successful group of promoters called The Best of Friends (TBOF). The Twins eventually managed Justine's, TBOF's second club in Manhattan. TBOF had Leviticus for the older crowd, while The Dow Twins' managed Justine's for the younger, post-college students. These were the hottest Black discos around, and the partnership helped to corner the market. The formation of this very lucrative merger brought Justice Vasquez, as well as me, into Norman and Harold's life.

Vincent Scott
Lifelong friend

THE DOW TWINS' LEGACY

The Move to Manhattan

After graduation from St. John's, my brother and I booked our first Manhattan event at Pippin's Nightclub on East 54th Street. It was *the* place to dance. It was a pre-holiday party, and perfectly timed to bring out a large crowd. The club was packed, the DJ was rocking, and the bartenders were busy serving drinks. Suddenly, while working the front door, I got pushed from behind. I was busy trying to collect door fees and make change, so I ignored it at first. But then there was another shove, and I had to stop for a second to see what was going on behind the curtain that separated the club interior from its entrance.

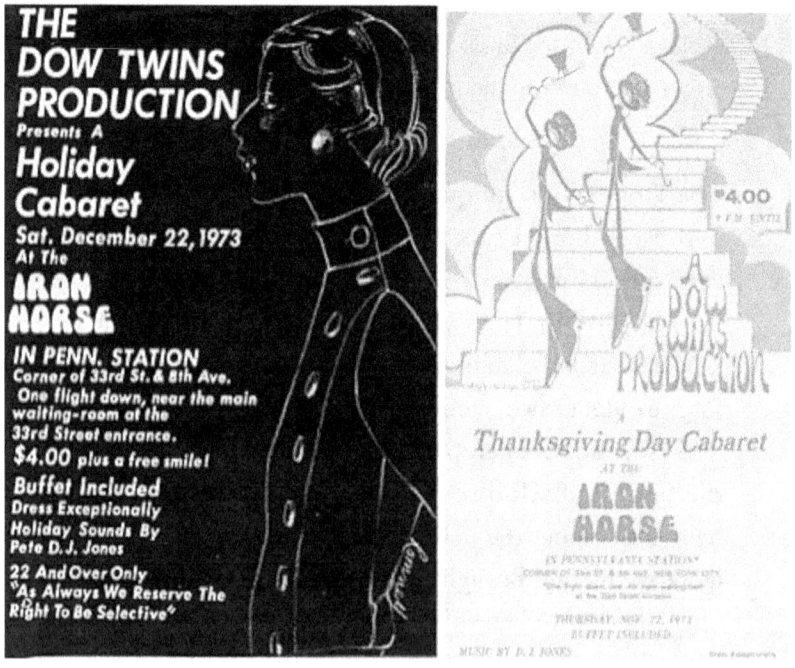

Early New York City promotional flyers

As I pulled back the drape behind me, I realized that the venue was so jam-packed that people were partying right up to the front door. There was no more room anywhere. We actually had to close the door and turn away many friends due to the throng. Now *that's* a successful party! The Pippin's event was a great moment for us and a fit reward for the countless hours we'd spent preparing, the numerous folks we'd invited, and the mass promotional mailings and handouts we'd organized. Our strategy had surely worked, and we were on our way.

> I must start by saying WOW! My relationship with The Twins goes back to when Harold and Norman graduated from Saint John's University, when they were giving waistline parties. Well, you know, at that time, no one would ever accuse Harold and Norman of being "Hip!" Yes, they were square, literally and figuratively, but a lot of fun.
>
> After college, my brother Ronnie split the scene for Paris to play pro basketball. So, I ended up hanging out weekly with Harold and Norman, and we did that for years. Our mothers, along with Justice's mom, had also become very good friends as well. We were like a family.
>
> The thing that I dug about The Twins was that they were not as provincial as most Queens folks. They didn't just identify with the borough of Queens. They had already visited Howard University and all the local colleges in the area, where they'd given themed events while still students themselves. They even made it down to Tennessee State (where Oprah and I were undergraduates).

There were always good times, from the Hamptons to Martha's Vineyard, from Bed Sty to Harlem and the Bronx.

Harold and Norman never had a "real job" (as we would say), but all the places that we'd go almost every week, from a street fair to judging a swimsuit competition, helped to develop The Dow Twins' brand prior to them coming on board at Othello (later renamed Justine's). Because of Harold and Norman, Justine's became a huge success. Young Black urban professionals would frequent Justine's because it was not a pretentious environment. The Twins would just make everyone feel special. They even gave events at Leviticus for the NY Knicks and others—all while doing big things at Justine's during the week and on the weekends. Other Black promoters would ask, "What are you guys doing here? Aren't you supposed to be at Justine's?" Their answer would be, "Just supporting other Black businesses!"

Some promoters did show a little jealousy. It was once said to me that, "Your boys are parking two Mercedes convertibles directly in front of their club; ain't cool man!"

I believe that The Twins were somewhat responsible for the Black and Latin American community partying together again, like they did in the sixties: *Salsa Fridays* at Justine's. Need I say more! From Eddie Palmieri and Ray Barreto to Bobby Rodriguez and Bailor, it was caliente!

Ray James
The "Marathon Man"

Norman, Harold and I grew up together, graduated from high school, and went on to the same college. Then we went our separate ways, and I didn't see them for several years. Next thing I knew, my friends were all raving about these guys from Queens who were twins on the cutting edge, doing these fabulous New York events like pool parties, happy hours, etc. Apparently their parties were the place to be. I kept hearing about "The Twins"—these handsome, charming young men who were all the rage. Finally, someone put a name to them for me … The Dow Twins! My first thought was, "You've GOT to be kidding me!" The childhood pals whom I'd completely ignored were suddenly all the rage. They were no longer chubby boys, but handsome and full of charisma with those winning smiles! All of a sudden, I became very popular with my girlfriends because I knew them and could manage VIP access. They became the center of our social lives, wherever their events happened to be. They also became my overly-protective big brothers, with an opinion on every guy that I met at one of their events!

Barbara Cheives
Lifelong friend

Even when it snowed, Norman and I managed to draw huge crowds. Our next event was staged at a bar-restaurant called The Iron Horse located inside Penn Station—the main NYC train station on 34th Street and Eighth Avenue. Norman had nurtured a business relationship with the management and convinced them to close the bar on a Saturday night when there would be fewer travelers than during the week, and no afterwork crowd. We turned the space into a disco, offering dancing and finger food.

Our promotion strategy seemed strong, but that evening it began to snow just at the time when folks would be coming into the city for the party. Norman and I debated about shutting things down because, at this early stage of our careers, we didn't have advance ticket sales. We were nervous that folks might not show up in big numbers, despite our promotional efforts. This was an ongoing anxiety with our disco parties back then, which we held most weekends in the 1970s. Norman and I did not have a nine-to-five job and couldn't count on a bi-weekly paycheck. Nothing was guaranteed for entrepreneurs like us.

But that night at the Iron Horse, we were with a mentor—an NYPD gold shield officer named Bob Cagle. He reminded us that people of color tended to arrive late to parties and encouraged us not to shut the party down, but instead to put on our game face and to "never let them see you sweat," especially at the start of an event.

Sure enough, he was right. When folks began flowing in despite the snow, we were ecstatic, and we asked them, "Did you drive in from your home in the snow?" They told us, "No. We took the train in." Of course, they did! The party was in the train station! Duh! Soon enough, the party was on, and it turned out great. Management was happy, and Norman signed us up for multiple future dates. Sadly, we were only able to hold four more parties there before the venue was closed for renovations. Eventually, the Long Island Railroad Ticket Offices took over the space. Damn …

NEVER LET THEM SEE YOU SWEAT

Interior view of Othello

The Best of Friends:
Leviticus, Othello and Justine's

Our foray into Manhattan turned out to be a major source success in the 1970s. The White owners of the Iron Horse—the Reese Brothers—were so impressed by our ability to make money at the Iron Horse that they invited us to organize similar parties at their other restaurants, but we chose a different path. Instead, we became associated with another group of Black nightclub entrepreneurs: The Best of Friends (TBOF—the first successful Black discotheque owners in New York City). We had known some of the key members of TBOF from the St. Albans bowling alley in Queens where we all hung out.

TBOF was on the verge of opening the nightclub Leviticus on Sixth Avenue in 1975, and they needed a team to handle their other venue on Eighth Avenue—Othello (formerly a restaurant called The Brass Rail). They offered Norman and me an opportunity to manage the club and to create a social networking and dancing venue for Black college students, graduates, and their friends. Since TBOF's Leviticus clientele was four to six years older than us, we created a more relaxed, college-friendly party environment at Othello.

The rest is history. Leviticus became the place to be for the mature adults and Othello, soon to become Justine's, became the "spot" for a relaxed and younger audience. In addition to parties, Othello hosted all manner of events such as fashion shows and even children's parties. This opportunity to work with TBOF allowed us to help create and run a thriving business. We were in the right place at the right time and, as a result, we would go on to enjoy a most promising career in New York and, later, nationwide.

I was a founder of The Best of Friends (TBOF) in 1968 and helped create discotheques in New York City. When we opened Leviticus at 45 West 33rd Street in Manhattan on November 14th, 1974, it was an instant success. With lines down the block, we moved quickly to build another club in midtown. That's when we built Othello (later renamed Justine's). We were concerned about cannibalizing our great success at Leviticus, so Tony Cooper and Danny Berry, two of my partners in TBOF, came up with what turned out to be a brilliant idea: get The Dow Twins to manage Othello and bring in their crowd.

I'd heard of The Dow Twins in the early 1970s but didn't really meet them until 1975 when Tony and Danny introduced me. They were about five years younger than the members of TBOF and, importantly, they had a strong following that was younger than the average Leviticus patron. Eventually, most of our clientele went to both clubs and decided which environment they preferred. Each club had its own personality and style, but both had a strict dress code and required appropriate behavior once inside the club.

I was periodically embarrassed because it was difficult for me to tell The Twins apart. I relied on differences in facial hair, but they both made occasional changes, so it threw me off.

The Dow Twins were superior promoters—better than TBOF in many ways. They had a tremendous following and a great personal rapport with most of their guests.

Through the years of the relationship between TBOF and The Dow Twins, there was complete trust and honesty. The Dow Twins were extraordinarily reliable and knew how to solve problems. They never came to TBOF with issues—if there was a problem, they came up with solutions. That is a characteristic of a successful entrepreneur. It made life easy for all of us in TBOF and led to a success that lasted thirteen years. That's a longer lifespan than most nightclubs or discotheques. It's fair to say that TBOF would not have prospered as well without The Dow Twins.

Noel Hankin

Author of "After Dark: Birth of the Disco Dance Party"

Othello was a successful nightclub that attracted lots of women. Our formula for this was to always be protective of the ladies that frequented the club. Once the ladies entered, we considered them our responsibility.

On one occasion, for example, we were alerted by a customer that a man was insulting the women seated in a row of chairs facing the dance floor. I spoke to our security guy, "Batman," who was a 6' 5" body builder and a black belt, and who used to work one of the worst bars in New York City—the "Terminal Bar" at the Port Authority Bus Station. While Norman and I confronted the insulting patron and asked for his ID, Batman grabbed him by the back of his collar. With his other hand, Batman grabbed a hand full of the man's genitals from behind, causing him to start walking on tiptoe, right past the very ladies he had just insulted and out of Othello. It was an unforgettable and spontaneous move by Batman; and it reminded our customers that we always had their safety in mind.

Robert Gaines & Neal's Fashion Show at Othello

On another occasion, two women (who had heard the DJs on radio station WBLS talking about Othello) decided to see Othello for themselves on a Saturday night. Driving in from Connecticut, they parked a couple of blocks north of the club.

I was chatting with them later that night as they were about leave the club, and they told me where they had parked, on 37th Street near Ninth Avenue. I said, "Really? That's not a safe area at this time of night." And, of course, I offered to walk them back to their car.

THE DOW TWINS' LEGACY

Our Children's Holiday Party hosted by Othello's staff

As we walked, they noticed that I had positioned myself on the inside (not outside) of the street and asked why. Just then a homeless man stumbled out a dark doorway right next to me; he was harmless, but he scared the hell out of us. That's how their question was answered. You never knew who or what might jump out of a dark alley near Hell's Kitchen in the 1970s. Enough said.

In the days of Othello, the disco era was still hot. Dance clubs were everywhere. To this day none of us knows how the famous pop artist Andy Warhol found his way to Othello, which was near Madison Square Garden on the West Side; but he showed up and partied with us one Thursday night. At this time, the trend was for celebrities (White or otherwise) to come through and dance with Black folks. We had some of the younger New York Knicks visit, as well as Black jazz violinist Noel Pointer, and boxer Joe Frazier. Celebs like these loved that no one paid any attention to them, but just treated them like fellow partygoers. This may be why Warhol came back the following week with an entourage of his friends. It was all about the *party!*

Pop artist Andy Warhol, Italian fashion designer Valentino, actress Elizabeth Taylor and the Dow Twins at Othello. Photo: Alix DeJean

When I saw that Warhol was back with a group, I didn't even look twice until I heard a buzz going through the room. That's when I saw him dancing with a woman and knew immediately who she was—Elizabeth Taylor, and fashion designer Valentino! As the night went on, Norman noticed that they were getting ready to leave and he said, "Let's walk them out to make sure they get a cab." While waiting for the cab, photographer Alix Dejean, who had just walked over from Leviticus a few blocks away, arrived and asked to take a photo. Liz Taylor said, "Sure!" and grabbed Norman's hand. A historic photo was the result, taken under the Othello awning. How about that!

In 1975, Norman and I helped to renovate Othello with Tony Cooper of TBOF. Tony's father was a professional theater set designer who had also helped build out Leviticus as well as a third TBOF venue in Midtown East called Bogard's. If Norman and I had not lost enough weight already, we lost even more running up and down the stairs during the Othello renovation, carrying equipment, supplies, furniture, and so forth.

When the renovations were complete, TBOF renamed the club Justine's. They had negotiated a thirteen-year lease on both the Justine's and Leviticus locations, and at a very reasonable price because, at that time, the city was broke and Midtown West (especially Eighth Avenue where Justine's was located), was a "No Man's Land" of crime and prostitution.

It was a real challenge to get people to come to Justine's, but Norman and I were up for it. Once renovations were done, we outfitted the club with backgammon tables to entertain and attract classy clientele. More importantly, we hired an amazing young woman who would become an integral part of our business and lives for the next forty-plus years—Justice Vasquez.

> I came to Othello in 1975 to work the coatroom. In April, I realized that, because the weather was warming, there wouldn't be any more coats to check, and I'd be out of a job. So, I made myself useful. I suggested that I help create an office space at the club; I learned how to work the bar; and so it went … I kept learning from The Twins, and I enjoyed every minute of it. I was amazed at the loyalty of their customers, who seemed to all be people they knew personally.
>
> Over time, I became a part of their team. I often worked the door at The Twins' venues and had to appear tough so that no one tried to get in without paying. I also had to keep Norman and Harold's "people" separate in my

mind when I greeted them. Their special guests always got special treatment.

A few years later in 1980, when I left Norman and Harold at Justine's to work with Tony Cooper at the TBOF venue, Bogard's, I felt bad; but Norman and Harold were not far behind. They eventually partnered with members of TBOF but, before this at Justine's, TBOF owned the club and Norman and Harold managed it.

The best thing that could ever have happened to me was working with The Dow Twins and The Best of Friends. I was the only female around these ten guys who made me feel protected and safe from the hazards of the New York City club scene, like drugs and crime.

Justice Vasquez

Thanks to Justice, TBOF, and the rest of our team, Justine's was almost immediately a big hit, packing in crowds after work and on weekends. One of Justine's most successful campaigns was the introduction of "Salsa Fridays" in 1983 to attract the Latin-friendly crowd. In fact, in October of that year, Salsa Fridays presented "Reuben Blades Live" as a special treat for our clientele. On these nights, I handled the money and Norman handled the Latin ladies and other duties as the host.

I used to call Norman "Rodriguez" and Harold "Schwarz" [after the famed dancers]. Norman loved and appreciated women (especially Latina women), salsa music, salsa dancing and all things Puerto Rican.

Celebrating our 5th anniversary and get-well salute to a Salsa Friday's patron at Justine's

While I was dating Harold, Justice and I became close—so much so that when she left Justine's to manage a new TBOF dinner club, Bogard's, she put me in her seat as assistant manager at Justine's. But as a newbie, there was one incident which could have put the kibosh on my fledgling nightclub career.

Tasked with taking inventory at the bar, I was to note how much liquor was used and match this with the receipts of drinks sold. Okay (BTW, I also had to clean the meters, which provided measured shots each time). Determined to do a really good job, I was industriously cleaning all the meters with soap and really hot water until Justice said, "What are you doing?"

"Oh, cleaning the meters," I explained.

"Make sure you only use cold water, because the meters have plastic parts that will get damaged by hot water."

Nooooo! I pretty much ruined a bunch of expensive bar meters. I thought I was getting fired in my first few days. But no; I didn't get fired. Instead, Tony Cooper, Danny, Harold and Norman never let me forget it, and I became the butt of a bunch of jokes...

Also, Justice and I were the founding members of W.A.M! (Women Against Men), an in-house running joke that gave us so many hours of conversation and gut-busting laughter. It was hilarious.

❦

Dawn Steward Walton

Justine's was an unqualified success for over a decade. Day after day, week after week, and year after year, it was the "go-to" club for urban Black professionals and celebrities, as the recollections of our patron's attest.

Out of all The Dow Twins clubs, Justine's was my favorite back in the day. I loved it because you could go there after work and, at other times, party at night. We would always have a good time and dance to wonderful music. One of my experiences that I will never forget is that I met my husband there on Thanksgiving eve in 1978.

I loved Justine's. You never knew who you would run into. I met Rick James and the Pointer Sisters. Jose Dozier used to work at the door, and we became very good friends. Especially when he became popular on a show on TV called "Soap Factory Disco Show."

Harold and I became very close through a girlfriend of mine, who he allowed to have a roller-skating party inside Justine's, and we all had lots of fun. My friendship with Harold has grown over the years, and I love him dearly. I sold tickets for lots of his events and helped him out in whatever areas he needed me. He knows I will always have his back.

Virgie Baptiste
Salon Owner & Ticket Outlet in Harlem

Justine's also had an open-door policy when it came to renting the club to outside groups. On one occasion, when an LGBTQ+ organization known as Cinnamon Productions (made up primarily of Black lesbians) asked to rent the club for a Monday evening event, we were happy to accommodate them. At the time, Black lesbians were very much "underground," and this occasion was the first time Cinnamon Productions had been able to openly party at a traditional nightclub in Midtown. They requested that we provide female or gay male bartenders and that the party be by invitation only (no outsiders). Since we were normally closed on Monday's, this posed no problem.

Harold and Norman checking-out with bartender Jeff Brooks

Wanda and sister, modeling at Othello

NEVER LET THEM SEE YOU SWEAT

Pacho's Dance party with Chaka Khan at Justine's, 1978

Kneeling (L to R): Mike Glenn, WBLS' Vaughn Harper, Frankie Crocker, Ken Webb. *Standing (L to R):* Knicks Ken Houston and Hollis Copeland, Sportscaster Cal Ramsey, Knicks Earl Monroe, Ray Williams, and Michael Ray Richardson, NBC's Melba Toliver, Detroit Pistons' Bob McAdoo, Norman Dow, MSG's Paulette Lemelle, Harold A. Dow. *Printed in City Lights, March 1980*

As the party got underway, the invitees seemed to be having a great time. The music was flowing, and the dance floor was crowded. Soon, though, one of the hosts asked if Norman and I could leave for a while. When we gave her a puzzled look, she explained that some folks were staying outside because they didn't want to be seen (or identified) by us. Of course, we understood. Some of the women in their group might also be Justine regulars who knew us. We didn't want to make anyone who might be struggling with their sexual identity feel uncomfortable, so we both agreed to leave and let Justice Vasquez, our one-time-coat-check-girl-turned-assistant manager, handle the remainder of the evening, which went off without a hitch.

NEVER LET THEM SEE YOU SWEAT

Wow, the awesome memories of Justine's on a Friday or a Saturday night. Great memories that I will cherish always. It was as if time had the ability to pause when you were there. I felt excitement all day leading up to the parties I'd be going out to later that night. I often went shopping all day looking for just the right outfit to set it off. You didn't want to show up unless you were looking fly!

The music was always just the right mix for a boogie down great time. There was laughter, fun, meeting new people and often seeing an old friend you hadn't seen in years. The experiences you had at the parties were good, wholesome entertainment, and when it was time to go home many of us would be asking our friends, "Are you coming next week?" To which most would say "Yes," and we would look forward to meeting up again the following weekend for another fabulous time.

I met Norman and Harold at college. We all attended St. John's University. Harold and Norman soon became great friends and were like the brothers you would hope for. They were just the nicest gentlemen I had ever met in my younger years.

I had the honor and privilege of putting together several fashions shows with The Dow Twins at both Justine's and The Red Parrot. There was busy excitement behind the scenes as the designers and models prepared their hair, makeup and outfits. The Dow Twins' following were folks who had a great sense of style, and many were trendsetters. Often there were celebrities in our midst, so we did not want to disappoint. I can remember sitting at a table with my friends and just across from us Sidney Poitier and Harry Belafonte were seated at a table enjoying themselves. Many times, Eddie Murphy and his friends were in attendance. You came out expecting the unexpected, and you left having experienced just that!

Cathy Shuemate
Friend and supporter

Prestige 100 Honors presents awards to Pierre Sutton and Melba Toliver with Harold Dow, Dawne Steward, Bill McCreary and Norman Dow

Smiles all around as Norman cracks jokes at Othello during the holidays with twins Andrea and Annette Barker & bandaged Harold Dow

NEVER LET THEM SEE YOU SWEAT

This is the story of the nightclub entertainment world, of Black excellence, and of people going out to the best events and parties. It's about the dresses, the cars, the colognes—the whole story of what Black nightlife was in the '70s, with all the disco music that was coming out at the time.

My name is Melvin Scott Bryant. I started my nightclub career in Charles's Gallery—Charles Huggins' nightclub (the husband of singer/actress Melba Moore). Charles had a beautiful supper club, nightclub, and restaurant all combined in one. In 1974, I went into the restaurant to get something to eat. Everybody had told me how good the food was, but I didn't know that they had a nightclub in there. So, one day, I was in there ordering food when people started asking who I was. I told them that I worked at Ronnie's Casuals (a clothing store nearby on 125th Street in Harlem), and they said, "Oh yeah, yeah. I knew I saw you somewhere before." Charles and a couple of other people said that they had seen me around, too. That's how I met Charles and started working in his nightclub.

I really wanted to work there because it was filled with beautiful people; and for a Black man to own such a beautiful nightclub at that time was very revolutionary. It had glass; it had tablecloths; it had waiters; it was a beautiful, upscale bar that radiated excellence. And this was in Harlem—315 West 125th Street, between 8th and Saint Nick. It was the old Frank's restaurant that had been taken over by Charles Huggins, and he did a beautiful job making it over.

So, when I started working there, Charles came up to me and said, "Scotty, I'd like you to do a night in Charles Gallery."

So, I said, "I know a lot of people, but I don't know if I can give a party."

Charles talked me into it. He said, "Scotty, a lot of people know you and like you, and they're gonna come."

So, going forward, I made up my first flyers. The party was called "Wild Wednesday," and it was during the week. At that time, Charles did not have a club night during the week when people would dance on a Wednesday or Tuesday. So, we started "Wild Wednesday," and we packed them in. It was crazy.

I got into Justine's (at that time it was called Othello) after a young lady outside of Charles's Gallery said to me, "You know, there's a beautiful club in Midtown and it's really nice." I had no idea what she was talking about, but it turned out that she was talking about Othello. "It's a Black-owned club and it's in Midtown." Back then, 125th Street held reign in the Black club scene. We had it locked down. But these guys—The Best of Friends and The Dow Twins—were in Midtown. So, I became interested in working with The Dow Twins.

By the time I approached Tony Cooper and Harold Dow, Herman M. and I had another club that was running successfully. Tony said to me, "Listen, I'm setting up a meeting and I want you to be there, Scotty. I'm spending a lot of money on a new club. I'm redoing Othello, and it's going to be called Justine's. I want you to come and have a night here."

I told my partner Herman, and he said, "Scotty, let's see what they're talking about." So, we had a meeting, and we decided to do an "after work" night. The Dow Twins sold me on the idea. I had never done an "after work." I'd heard about it, but I didn't know how successful it could be. I knew that Herman and I could do a 10:00 p.m. to 4:00 a.m., but never a Tuesday or Friday after work. It just wasn't in my vision; I couldn't put it together. But we went forwards anyway, and it came out very successfully.

The first inkling that I had that our venture was successful was on the evening of our first after-work party. I was living downtown at 40 Harrison Street. There was a guy named José who worked the front door at Justine's, and I called him to say, "José, I'm running a little bit late, but I'm on my way down there." It was about 6:30 p.m.

José said, "Scotty, you'd better get here fast."

I said, "Well, what's wrong?"

And he answered, "Man, there's a line outside going down Eighth Avenue."

I said, "Are you kidding me?"

He said, "Scotty, there's a line outside that's building up."

So, I shot up Hudson Street to 35th Street and Eighth Avenue and, by the time I got there, the place was packed and people were swarming in. I was just amazed, because

I never knew that people came out to party straight after work. But it was working. It was a success.

Tuesday was taking off. We had the crowd going crazy on Tuesdays. This was the place to be and the reason I made the transition from Charles's Gallery to Justine's. It was Black-owned by The Best of Friends and managed by The Dow Twins. So, I was very happy to be a part of that legacy because they were creating something historic. At that time WBLS, which was a Black-owned radio station that played Black music, was owned by Percy Sutton. Black radio station. Black nightclub. The promoters, Herman and I, were Black. It made total sense to me, and it really worked.

So, one Tuesday night I was standing at the bar, and at that time the disco group Chic was really hot. Their music was on fire: every club was playing it; every radio station was playing it. I knew the lead singer, Nile Rodgers, in the past but I had not seen him since he'd become a successful record producer. He walked right into Justine's with bandmates Bernard (who I also knew) and Tony. So, there was Nile Rogers, Bernard Edwards, Tony (who was their drummer) and the two female vocalists—the whole group, Chic, walked right in the front door of Justine's. It was jam-packed, and I was loving it. Nile stopped to talk to me, and I told him, "Nile, this is my party tonight."

He said, "This is your party? Great. Great. This is cool."

We started talking about how he was doing things in in a big way. He told me that he was working on Diana Ross' new album, and he had a track on it called "I'm Comin' Out" (which he and Bernard Edwards wrote and produced, and which hit #5 on the Billboard charts before becoming an historic LGBTQ+ anthem).

I was impressed. "Wow, you're producing Diana Ross? That's big." He told me that he met with Berry Gordy and that he and Bernard were going to produce the album. He also told me about a young Caucasian lady he was working with. "I'm putting a lot of money in her, man," he said.

I asked, "Well, how does she sound?"

And he said, "She sounds good, you know, but I'm just putting in so much of money; and I'm going to be producing her." Later on, that young lady would go on to become Madonna. They just didn't have the name for her as of yet.

So, on this particular Tuesday night when Nile Rodgers and Chic came to Justine's, I felt very, very excited to have "Black excellence" in the club, partying with the people. They weren't at Studio 54. They were at Justine's. At that time, Chic's music was being played in every club around the country. They were on fire. So, the fact that people like Nile Rodgers was walking through the front door on a Tuesday night was really big to me. I told, Nile, "I gotta recognize you guys while you're here."

And, he said, "Yeah, Scotty, no problem, no problem."

So, I told him to, "Just sit tight." I wanted the people to know that Chic—the complete group—was in the house.

I had the DJ stop the music and announced to the crowd, "Listen, can we get Chic to come in the middle of the floor?

Will you give them a round of applause?" The audience loved it, because they knew Chic. They'd heard their music, but they couldn't believe that the group was right there partying with them. Everyone went crazy. And behind them was Sarah Dash of LaBelle, who had a hot record out at that time, too. So now you have Sarah Dash and the whole complete group Chic hanging out, Tuesday night.

It was Black excellence. It was royalty. And they were partying with the people: that was the best part, the most exciting thing. Of course, there was the Phyllis Hyman story when she came in. Then there was Rick James when he was partying at Justine's. But those are other stories...

Melvin Scott "Flash" Bryant
Promoter and friend for fifty years

Celebrating with Scotty Bryant, singer Sarah Dash,
Harold Dow, Chic producer Nile Rodgers, MSG's Paulette Lemelle and
Norman Dow at Leviticus

Justine's was a small space compared to the immense size of Leviticus, where Norman and I hosted themed parties for larger crowds. Some of the key Leviticus events were the Prestige 100 Honors (The Dow Twins' VIP Clientele) for radio executive Pierre "Pepe" Sutton (son of civil rights activist Percy Sutton), journalist Melba Tolliver, and the New York Knicks (1979); the Prestige 100 City Lights publication launch (which sold out in 1980); Prestige 100 Live, honoring Stephanie Mills (1980); The Dow Twins' "For Women Only" launch (our first male stripper review, which opened to standing room only in 1981); our Easter Sunday Fancy Dress Ball and Black Tie Gala (1981); The Dow Twins' 30th Gemini Birthday Party (1981); and the Prestige 100 event honoring banker Steve Roberts (1982). These are just a few of a series of highly successful Leviticus events.

But all was not roses at Othello, Justine's, and Leviticus. Given their locations, the clubs were prone to robberies. During the late 1970s while we were managing Othello, we believed that we had always treated our patrons with respect and decency. Apparently, though, we must have ruffled some feathers along the way, because early one evening two detectives from the Midtown South Precinct came to our office to inform us that, during a wiretap, they had heard a suspect identify Norman and I as targets of a "hit."

Since we knew a couple of brothers from that precinct, we thought it was a prank and laughed it off; until, a few days later, one of our staff members barged into our office with the same two detectives. They swarmed around us with guns in-hand and scared the hell out of our staffers. That's when we realized the threat was real. They had brought bullet-proof vests for us to wear, told us that they would be shadowing us for the next twenty-four hours, and instructed us not to tell anyone. Fortunately (and thanks to the NYPD), we were not killed, and nothing ever came of it.

Another incident occurred in October of 1983. Norman and I were awakened at our home by the fire department calling to inform us that the building at 500 Eighth Avenue (where Justine's was located) was on fire. Fortunately, the FDNY was on the scene and the fire was doused with only our office space destroyed. Nevertheless, this was a devastating loss of photos, records, and memorabilia that could never be recouped. We learned later that a bartender who had once worked for us was the culprit. He had robbed our office of cash and two Gold Albums by Stephanie Mills and funk band GQ, and then set the office on fire.

In a related incident on January 26th, 1984, two armed robbers caught the front door of Justine's before it locked behind our DJ Derrick, who had just left the building at 5:00 a.m. With gun in hand, the perpetrators came downstairs to our lower-level office, taking me and a waitress by surprise. They had the drop on us, but they didn't get much money because we had just paid the staff with the night's receipts. They checked the safe and saw that it was empty, so they started taking other things, including liquor and a small TV.

Next, they reached over me to rip the phones off the wall so we couldn't call the police. I said, "You don't need to do that," and gave him the headset from one phone and the cord from the other (I knew, but they didn't, that I could reassemble one phone with the remaining parts once they left—provided they didn't kill us).

While trying to calm our waitress, who was crying and screaming hysterically, I noticed that a third person was hiding behind the office door. I thought, "Who is that? Is he hiding so we won't ID him?" As he signaled for his accomplices to lock us in the office, I caught a glimpse of him and saw that he was light skinned with a ponytail. He looked suspiciously like the same former bartender; and he was, as we would soon confirm.

Later that week, our other DJ, Reggie Wells, called just after leaving at closing time and said he'd seen our former bartender and his two likely accomplices hanging out near Sixth Avenue and 35th Street. Immediately, I drove to the police station a block away and reported the sighting. I thought the police were ignoring me, because they didn't seem to want to take any action. So, I drove to the corner where Reggie had spotted the trio. With adrenaline coursing through my veins, I recognized the guy who had held the gun on us. He saw me, too, and ran up Seventh Avenue.

I headed after him, actually driving the wrong way down Seventh Avenue so as not to lose him. Fortunately, at 6:00 a.m. there was no traffic. I had almost pinned him to a storefront gate when I heard sirens blaring behind me. *Yes*, the police had been following me the whole time, and arrested him on the spot. All three of them were tried and found guilty.

Even though it was in a somewhat better location, Leviticus was not exempt from crime either. One night, I had come over to Leviticus from Justine's and saw TBOF member, Charles "CP" Perry, standing behind the bar and walked over to greet him. As we used to say, "the joint was jumping"—until we heard a shotgun blast—BOOM! BOOM!—and everybody started running towards the exit at the back of the club. That's when a man, who had been shooting up at the ceiling, jumped over the bar where CP and I were into the bartender's pit, where the cash registers were located. He looked right at us and said, *"Didn't I tell you to get down on the floor?!"*

With that, we immediately ate carpet. CP and I looked at each other, and it seemed we were watching a scene out of a movie. Meanwhile, regulars and celebrity guests alike (including Soul Train's Don Cornelius) were running for their lives. They emptied the registers, then mugged some patrons on their way out.

After they'd gone, we couldn't believe what had just happened right in front of our eyes. After calling the police and tending to some of the patrons, we noticed that there was no damage to the ceiling. It turns out that the thieves were shooting blanks the entire time. Still today, I recall this night with amazement.

Another potential robbery was thwarted by two NYPD Black police officers—Harvey Erwin and his partner Mel Doby, who frequented Leviticus:

> The fact of the matter is that all the nights I spent at Leviticus are memorable. But this night stands out amongst the others. It was in 1978. It was a very hot Friday night; Mel Doby and I were scheduled to work a four-to-twelve tour at the 76 Precinct. At around 12:00 a.m. that day we decided to take a few hours, have dinner, and go to Leviticus.
>
> After dinner, we parked our car and walked on the north side of the street towards Leviticus. As we got closer to the club, we observed two Black men standing in a doorway across the street, partially hidden by cars and shadows. We could hear one of the men say, "Wait till they get inside." We looked towards the club and saw that there were several couples waiting to get in. Then we looked back at the two men. What was strange about

them was that, as hot as it was, both were wearing long, black trench coats.

As one of the men stepped out of the doorway, he adjusted his coat, and protruding from it was a sawed-off shotgun that dangled from a shoulder strap. The second man came out of the doorway adjusted his coat, showing a shotgun as well. Mel and I stayed hidden behind a parked van. The men moved completely out of the doorway, placed themselves behind a car and eyed the club as they closed their trench coats. It was clear that they were waiting for the last people to enter Leviticus before making their move. We had to stop them before that happened. There was still time.

The last few people were still at the door. Mel ran to the corner to a phone booth (no cell phones then) and placed a call to the Midtown South Precinct. They, in turn, notified an anticrime team that was only two blocks away. The anticrime team of four arrived in two unmarked cars just in time; two couples were still waiting to enter the club. Mel met with the team and explained the situation.

The anticrime team waited until Mel got back to my location. The strategy was to move in very quickly and take the men by surprise; and we did just that. As Mel and I came from behind the van and moved towards the two men, the crime teams in the unmarked cars pulled up at the same time. There was a slight struggle, but the men were down on the ground in handcuffs before they realized what hit them. Both were carrying shotguns and .38 caliber handguns. No shots were fired, and I think only a couple of people at Leviticus heard the scuffle as they were going into the club.

Both men had extensive criminal records. They were charged with carrying concealed weapons—a felony because of their records—and were sentenced to more than ten years. Anytime you make an arrest like this, and no shots are fired, the police department rewards you nicely. Mel and I were not looking for accolades that night, so we just settled for the assist; after all, we had taken time off from work to do one thing—party at Leviticus. We were at the right place at the right time.

Mel and I agreed that two men who really deserved an award were Harold and Norman. They brought to New York something new and exciting. They were great hosts; and the atmosphere was beautiful as well as the people. I've said it before: they must have gone out and hand-picked the most beautiful women in New York and the surrounding area. Fantastic job!

And, as always, we had another fantastic night at Leviticus mingling with the people and dancing the night away. Well, Norman and Mel are gone now, but the great memories I have of Harold, Norman, Mel, Justice, and Leviticus will last forever. Once again, I thank you so much.

Harvey Erwin

In typical "New York cool" fashion, after their ordeal, officers Erwin and Doby simply went into Leviticus and commenced to party—not once (until now) mentioning their heroics.

Justine's and Leviticus thrived for thirteen years—a decade longer than Studio 54—and yet the mainstream media knows very little about these iconic venues. Our clientele was protected from drugs, exclusionary practices, and high prices—something Studio 54 and clubs like it did not always achieve. They were often expensive, drug-friendly, and equipped with "selectors" at the door who would decide if you were good enough get in.

After such a long and successful run, it was, nevertheless, a relief to eventually say goodbye, because my brother and I had been solely responsible for Justine's, including liquor and supply stock, payroll, staff, promotion, maintenance, cleaning, security—our years there involved a lot of hard work and little time off. We learned from this experience that we much preferred "pop-up" venues, where we could rent a space for a night and move on without the worries associated with a permanent site. One-offs were definitely easier and no less profitable. Also, not all of our clientele liked to go to the same spot over and over again. They preferred variety.

So, in late 1985, we decided to cut ties with Justine's. By then, our only stationary location was a bar and restaurant that Norman and I had opened, along with Justice, Tony Cooper, and Danny Berry, in our old neighborhood in Queens—Manhattan Proper Café.

CHAPTER THREE

The Formula For Bringing People Together

1980s Hit Songs

"Let's Groove" by Earth, Wind & Fire

"Rock Steady" by The Whispers

"I Wanna Dance with Somebody" by Whitney Houston

༄

Manhattan Proper Café

In 1985, shortly before Justine's closed, Norman, Justice Vasquez and I opened Manhattan Proper Café in Queens (later, The Proper Café). We partnered with TBOF members Tony Cooper and Danny Berry in a space that had originally been a Chase Bank. Tony and Danny, who had been friends since the third grade, had decided to separate from TBOF, and they saw Manhattan Proper as their opportunity to do so; and Justice had a friend willing to lend her some investment cash. We hired new staff to help run it and—voilà—it all came into place. The thought of an upscale restaurant and meeting place in Queens Village excited us all. Norman and I had grown up in the area, and many of the folks from our multiple events in the city lived there, too.

We planned for Manhattan Proper Café to bring an upscale dining experience to the family and friends we grew up with. It was a no brainer. For ten years we'd been focused on Manhattan, but the Manhattan clubs were about to end their leases. Also, Norman and I wanted to move back to our original format of "one off" affairs. No longer tied to Justine's, we now had the time and resources to bring a great meeting and dining place to our own neighborhood. With the team we had and the number of people we collectively knew, the odds of success were in our favor. The venture coincided with our mom having a little health scare, so it was an ideal time for Norman and me to start a business in Queens to be near her.

Now the fun part started: re-outfitting and branding our new bar and restaurant and bringing an upscale dining experience to the area. Justice and the chefs designed a wonderful array of foods for our menu, which was deliberately small so that it could be run by just a few partners. This made it possible for me to focus my attention on other ventures—The Dow Twins' Printing and Marketing business, which we opened on West 36th Street, and our ongoing "pop-up" events.

This arrangement allowed each of us to shine in our respective areas of expertise. Norman was the manager of Manhattan Proper Café; Tony and Danny handled the bar; and Justice was co-manager in charge of the restaurant menu and services. Already close friends, as co-managers of Manhattan Proper, Justice and Norman became "besties."

Norman and Justice

I had an extremely special bond with Norman. I'd lost a brother in childhood, and The Twins had no sisters, so we filled a void for each other. Norman and I were inseparable, and he was very protective of me. In forty-seven years of friendship, we had no beefs, and we talked every day. Once at Manhattan Proper, I had to go to the bathroom while we were having a conversation, and he actually followed me into the bathroom rather than stop talking to me! I had to ask him to give me a minute before he reluctantly gave me some privacy.

Every Tuesday, we shopped together for the restaurant's kitchen. I spent the Sunday that Justine's closed at The Twins' house in Secaucus playing cards. We traveled together to Bermuda. We were just like siblings. Norman and Harold were Mets fans, but I was a Yankee fan, which made for a lively ongoing rivalry.

I never felt like a third wheel with The Twins. Although I lost my brother young, I gained two brothers with Norman and Harold.

Manhattan Proper Café was very important to Norman—more so than Justine's because he had become an owner. Prior to that, he was essentially an employee of TBOF. Norman worked the door at Manhattan Proper and people loved coming there. He made sure that everything went right.

The interior of Manhattan Proper Café
during the Christmas Holidays

I cared more about Manhattan Proper, too. Norman and I had the same vision. For instance, when Tony Cooper and his wife were about to get married, I gave Diane a bridal shower at Manhattan Proper. I came in one day before the shower and found Norman painting the walls. When I asked, "What are you doing?" He said that he wanted to make the place look great for the shower (he broke his leg falling off the ladder and was out of commission for a while. I felt so guilty). That's how Norman was. If I had a vision and talked to him about it, he would make sure it was achieved. For example, during the holidays, everything was decorated and looked excellent. He did whatever he could possibly do. I felt that he was so very proud of Manhattan Proper Café, as I was.

≈

Justice Vasquez

Norman loved fixing things. He was an avid gardener and, in his capacity as landlord to our property in Secaucus, New Jersey since 1984, his attention to detail in maintaining the house earned the admiration of our tenants. Initially, Norman had tried his best to convince me to purchase a property on Lafayette Avenue and Pineapple Street in the Brooklyn downtown area, but the reconstruction of a brownstone shell at such a busy time of our lives would have been impossible to handle, so we settled on the property in New Jersey.

At the same time, Norman got his real estate license and maintained an office for many years down the block from Manhattan Proper with Halmike Realty. His manager at Halmike, Debbie Younger, along with the Anderson family, who owned the agency, were truly big fans of Norman's personality and popularity. Norman enjoyed his role as a realtor, helping our friends and clientele to position their homes for sale. The only thing that slowed his sales record was the fact that some folks were very sensitive about their financial history and felt uncomfortable revealing it to Norman—someone they knew personally—which was necessary for any home sale. Norman understood their reluctance and kept moving forwards. He focused instead on those clients who had their finances well organized.

Prestige 100 Honors TV Newscaster & Mentor Bill McCreary with Steve Roberts and the Twins

The Manhattan Proper Café's opening ceremony was hosted by Emmy Award-winning television journalist Bill McCreary. We were lucky to know Bill McCreary and his wife, who was a good friend of my mother's. Bill suggested hosting his TV news show, The McCreary Report, from our restaurant as part of the launch. We were further honored by the community's ministers, who blessed the property, and by local politicians who helped open our doors.

Manhattan Proper Café offered patrons a diversity of fun experiences that my brother and I had become known for: ladies' nights, comedy shows, Monday Night Football, private parties, and jazz and karaoke nights. One of our favorite karaoke singers was a friend named Keisha White, who was a schoolteacher. She had a huge following and a great singing voice. In fact, so many people came out to hear her sing we had to hire extra staff on those nights, which were usually pre-holiday Sundays. Her "crew" of ladies would all show up with her, dressed in the color of the evening, which Keisha chose, and the party was on…

Manhattan Proper was the crown jewel of Queens. Anytime anyone had out-of-town visitors they would take them to Manhattan Proper, especially on Thursdays and Sundays when they had karaoke night. It was a down-home place where everyone felt safe, loved, entertained and cared for. They also had a world-famous menu, and people loved getting food there. There was always plenty of parking in a nearby supermarket lot, which we needed because there were so many patrons almost every day of the week.

You would walk in there and the bartenders would know you by name. Harold and Norman were amazing managers. Every time we looked around someone was throwing a party or event there. Karaoke was my special time of the week, because I got to sing other songs besides the gospel songs that I would sing in church. Often, I would bring out my ventriloquist puppet—a monkey named Jethro—and would sing to it "I Am Telling You I'm Not Going," which was a favorite and had everybody cracking up.

I will never forget Manhattan Proper. My twin sister Carlie and I very much enjoyed many years entertaining and being entertained there. There was no other place like it in the world.

Keisha White
Family friend

L I V I N G

DISHIN' IT OUT REVIEWS...
MANHATTAN PROPER CAFÉ
By Rainé H. Young

Hot pink on the outside with a cool pink interior, Manhattan Proper Cafe dishes out continental cuisine with a Southern flair in the middle-class neighborhood of Cambria Heights, Queens in New York City. "We chose pink because it's avant garde and our skin tones look good against pastel colors, which are light and bright and reflect a warm ambience," say the Dow Twins, who are one-third owners of Manhattan Proper, their latest business venture.

Perhaps some of you buppies remember the Dow Twins from the late '60s and early '70s when the focus of their entrepreneurism was the discotheque. Harold and Norman, together with the Best of Friends (the second third of Manhattan Proper's ownership), and Justice Vasquez (the last third) were the owners of the very popular black clubs Leviticus, Justine's and Bogard's. "We decided to reinvest in a restaurant instead of a club," says Norman. "After 12 to 15 years in that scene we wanted to bring back something to the community we grew up in. And the restaurant works here; we have the support of family and friends, and we have an older clientele [35 and up] who are looking for an opportunity to frequent a place such as this without going to Manhattan."

Don't let the location be an excuse to pass up a meal here. There is a convenient map on the back of the menu with directions, which makes Manhattan Proper easily accessible from all boroughs, Long Island and New Jersey.

Labeling the menu "continental cuisine with a Southern flair" brought alternative dining to the community and actually describes the food quite well. The combination of Robert Gaines (the downhome chef) and Barbara Whitfield (the gourmet) in the kitchen is excellent and they turn out scrumptious appetizers, soups, salads and entrees. Ordering the authentic hot and spicy Buffalo chicken wings is a natural. The house specials change daily; you'll be in luck if the perfectly seasoned duck with orange slices or pasta primavera with shrimp is one of them. An equally good entree is the Manhattan Proper Cordon Bleu stuffed with mozzarella cheese, with or without ham. Entrees come with potatoes or rice pilaf, steamed vegetables, and, if requested, hot apple spice muffins. A dessert special is fresh strawberries with Grand Marnier sauce.

Prices are moderate and Diners Club and AMEX are accepted. The restaurant is open for dinner only Wednesday through Sunday with a Southern brunch on Sunday. Jazz is the entertainment on Friday and Saturday and a late night menu is available on those nights from midnight to 3 a.m. "We're very popular—the food brings people back," the Dow Twins say proudly. "This is an anchor in the community. It's all fresh and that's the key." ■

A positive review of our new restaurant

THE FORMULA FOR BRINGING PEOPLE TOGETHER

Manhattan Proper Café was mainly Norman's project, rather than mine. He was the painter, the host, the gardener, the manager, Mr. Fix-it, decor specialist, sports geek, Mr. "Take off your hat, please!" and much more. If you needed something done, Norman was the *man*.

Most importantly, Norman handled the weekend door, which was critical to our success. He was there every day except Sundays when I came in to give him a break. I was the Sunday evening swing manager at The Proper for years, which was the day of the infamous "Karaoke Nights" hosted by Mark Rock, with chef Craig Canty providing those ever-popular buffalo wings and fried shrimp baskets.

As the "face" of Manhattan Proper Café, Norman sometimes had to play the "bad guy." This was needed along the Linden Boulevard bar strip. Locals were not accustomed to an upscale bar in their area, but we were determined that Manhattan Proper Café would be exactly that. As owners of the new bar/restaurant on Linden Boulevard, we tried to create an atmosphere similar to our city establishments.

For instance, during the first years of Manhattan Proper Café it was important to establish a dress code for the weekends—a policy that was not imposed by most other establishments in Southeast Queens. On the weekends, the code was no sneakers or jeans for men and ladies. It took a while, but the neighborhood eventually accepted it, though begrudgingly. It usually made working the door difficult, to say the least; but Norman remained firm with our door policy, using grace and diplomacy. Tony and Danny were also on board since they'd had a similar policy during their days with Lucifer's—the first TBOF club.

Gentlemen of The Proper Café showing off, Harold, Danny Tony, Herman, Evan, Duke and Norman

One of the outcomes of the dress code and of Norman's supervision of the door was that Norman became a sort of mentor to young men in the community who frequented Manhattan Proper Café. For example, one evening a young man, dressed in jeans, came to the door. Norman not only explained the dress code to him, but he assured him that the ladies inside were more accepting of a well-dressed man than one who looked like he had just finished playing ball with his friends. When the young man returned, properly dressed, Norman let him in for free and he had a great time.

Years later, not knowing that Norman had passed, he returned with his fiancée to introduce her to Norman and to thank him for his advice, which had changed the young man's outlook and life.

In 2001, Justice pulled off a surprise fiftieth birthday dinner party for Norman and me, and we were both really caught off

THE FORMULA FOR BRINGING PEOPLE TOGETHER

guard. Somehow Justice contrived to get Norman away from The Proper long enough to set up the room with formal assigned seating, a podium, and decorations. She also sent us on a fake trip to the city and back. It was a well-coordinated ruse, and her plan worked perfectly. The invitations read as follows:

> *NEWS FLASH:*
> *The Dow hits an all time high of 50! Harold & Norman celebrate half a century of twin ship.*
>
> *It's incredible but true; those dynamic Dow Twins are finally 50! But this blue chip duo shows no sign of splitting, quitting or slowing down. In fact their stock just keeps on rising as they continue to reign as two of New York's most successful entrepreneurs, promoters and men-about-town. We invite you to invest an evening in celebration of ths momentous Birthday. It's the A list, you're on it, there'll be wining and dining, toasting and teasing lots of laugh, and perhaps even a tear or two as we salsa down memory lane with New York's dynamic duo so come eat, drink and be merry and show them some love.*

The Dow Twins' 50th Surprise Invitation

Even when celebrities patronized Manhattan Proper Café, Norman held to the dress code.

When we first opened, our policy was "no hats" for men; and one night LL Cool J (who never took off his hat) came in. Norman explained the policy and LL said, "Do you know who I am?"

Norman answered, "Yes, I do." A little exchange took place between them. Norman would not let him in, and LL left. I believe that LL had respect for Norman for standing by his policy; word got around to any other men who wanted to wear their hats inside. If LL Cool J couldn't get in with a hat, what chance did they have? You can't always feel that you're going to get your way just because you're a celebrity (PS: LL did return on another occasion and kept his hat on).

I do feel that good customers got a pass sometimes, but it depended on what that pass was—a good table, food after the kitchen had officially closed … I think Norman was a very good host. Women loved coming there because they felt safe with him around. If he was there, they could sit at the bar and not worry about men hitting on them or being disrespectful because Norman would step to them and let them know that he didn't allow that.

Justice Vasquez

During its years in business, Manhattan Proper was the scene of many escapades. One, in particular, involved two of Norman's favorite customers, who just happened to be NYPD Emergency Service officers in Queens: Tony Anderson and his partner, Tito. They stopped by occasionally on their breaks, drawn to The Proper Café's friendly staff, delicious food, and Norman's warm personality and lively conversation.

Once during their shift, a lady from their precinct was celebrating her birthday at The Proper Café, and the Emergency Service duo stopped by to celebrate with her, bringing with them several other Black officers in their patrol cars. Norman went outside and, seeing so many police cars double parked, he realized that people would think The Proper Café was involved in a police action (especially given its corner location on the sometimes crime-prone Linden Boulevard). If that wasn't bad enough, Tony and Tito arrived in their huge Tactical Emergency Service vehicle. Alarmed, Norman shouted, "You guys have to go across the street to the supermarket's parking lot."

After a great laugh and hugs from the guys, they took their vehicles across the street. What a night!

NYPD Emergency Services Unit Detectives Tony and his partner Tito with Norman outside Manhattan Proper Café

The Proper Café thrived for over thirty-two years, but after Norman's passing in November 2005, it was just not the same. Some began to question the quality of the crowd; or maybe it was just the neighborhood changing. Norman's vigilance at the door was not shared by the new door staff. Long-term regulars were moving out of Queens and retiring to the milder southern states, such as Virginia, the Carolinas, and the Florida beaches.

THE DOW TWINS' LEGACY

The Proper Café now had new clientele. They still enjoyed the comedy, karaoke, and Monday night football gatherings, but not in the same numbers or with the same enthusiasm as they had before.

After Manhattan Proper Café closed in 2017, southeast Queens had become a ghost town in terms of any upscale, safe meeting places for those baby boomers who remained in the neighborhood. Not long ago, to my surprise, an older couple approached me as I was getting into my car and asked, "Where are we supposed to go now that Manhattan Proper has closed?"

I replied honestly, "When you find out where, please let me know. Really!"

The Manhattan Proper Café's Original 1985 Menu

THE FORMULA FOR BRINGING PEOPLE TOGETHER

> Norman brought a lot of pleasure and style to Manhattan Proper Café. It wasn't just another restaurant or club. It was "Manhattan Proper."
>
> Justice Vasquez

Despite its legacy, when Manhattan Proper Café closed there wasn't a whisper in the local news or trending websites sites about this thirty-two-year-old staple of the community. If this was Harlem, there would have been "outrage" that such a long-standing restaurant and meeting place was closing—and three or four bids from local investors to re-open or upgrade the facility would have followed. But the Café left a legacy, nevertheless.

> The people that worked for us at Manhattan Proper Café went on to do well. A couple of doctors came out of there. A lot of people kept up with us to tell us about their journeys in life. How much they miss Manhattan Proper because there was no place like it in that area to go anymore.
>
> I thought Manhattan Proper would last forever. But, two years after Norman's passing, Harold knew that it was time to close up shop. The end of an era.
>
> Justice Vasquez

The Manhattan Proper's early staff enjoying their successful Anniversary!

The ladies celebrating Mom: Natalie, Debora, Harold, Gloria, Renee & Wanda

THE FORMULA FOR BRINGING PEOPLE TOGETHER

The WWRL Years

As the 1980s moved into the '90s, "things they were a-changing" for me and my brother. While Norman directed his efforts into The Proper Café, I launched The Dow Twins' Design & Print business at the office suite of typesetter Bill Woods, graphic designer Lola Stephens, and commercial photographer Chris Gunzel on 36th Street and Seventh Avenue, half a block from Justine's.

With all the events we had been producing at Justine's, Leviticus, the other TBOF locations, and now Manhattan Proper, it only made sense to publish a newsletter about all our activities so our folks could keep up with what was going on. This allowed everyone to see what they had missed in previous months, and what they could look forward to in the future.

We started our first newsletter while we were still running Justine's and called it "City Lights" (later renamed "Sneak Preview"). In addition to feature stories and event information, it included half- and full-page ad placements by minority businesses in the tri-state area. "City Lights" was handed out at Justine's and other TBOF locations. Dawne Steward was writer and editor for the newsletter, and designers Bill Woods and Lola Stephens did the rest. Prior to its closing, the staff from Justine's helped with labelling and postage in their down time, making it truly a team effort.

Harold and I worked together every day in the office, and we began putting together marketing materials for the special events. This evolved into production of a small promotional magazine named "City Lights," for which I became the editor and senior copywriter. It was very successful; people liked it and eagerly sought to see their names and pictures in it, or to guess who was being "put on blast" in the blind items. It was fun, but more importantly it developed my writing chops and advertising portfolio, and it contributed to me getting my first professional job as a promotion copywriter at Time Inc.

Dawne Steward Walton
A cherished friend

Cover Shots of Sneak Preview and City Lights

Our mailers and brochures were key to keeping our advertising costs down since we received a very limited marketing budget while we were with TBOF. Mailers (as opposed to radio advertising) also kept public exposure to a controlled limit, which allowed us to maintain certain standards, including a dress code, age requirements, and upscale clientele. This strategy helped us to avoid many of the pitfalls that "open to the public" clubs experienced.

"City Lights" and "Sneak Preview" were well received due to their timeliness and the amount of helpful information on current happenings listed in each month's issue. In fact, one advertising client reported to us that our mailer had a four-to-one pickup value, which meant that in each home the mailer entered, it was referred to by the recipient(s) at least four times in deciding about places to go and things to do. *Thank You, Tri-State Area!*

I maintained my office at the 36th Street location for ten years until the building was sold. That's when my friend and General Manager of WWRL 1600 Radio, Adriane Gaines, invited me to join her team in Woodside, Queens. I don't remember how or even when Adriane and I met, but I always recall acknowledging her whenever we ran into each other, and she invariably asked about Norman and my mom whenever she saw me. So, when I told her one day that my 36th Street office was closing, she suggested coming out to WWRL's office in Woodside. Adriane told me that she handled the day-to-day business of the radio station there, and she thought the location could work for me and that I'd make a good promotional collaborator with the station.

Although I was thankful, I had become a bit of a Manhattan snob by this time and had to think about it. Soon enough, though, I agreed, and what a great decision it was for both of us. I used our massive database to inform our folks about a new music format being launched by WWRL; and their office suite provided a space for me to handle The Dow Twins' special events business.

At WWRL, I worked with Marko Nobles, the station's public relations specialist. I contributed to the marketing program and to the database of listeners to increase the station's outreach. I also assisted on some promotional activities at the station. One of the first was "The Soul City Music Series," a dance party held at various locations throughout the city.

We hosted the first one at Manhattan Center Studios on 34th Street and Eighth Avenue. The event was "standing room only." Ray, Goodman & Brown performed live, and the folks really enjoyed the musical selections of DJ Reggie Wells (formerly of Justine's). We were amazed when, during one of the high-energy soundtracks, the dance floor actually started to shake, which was a bit unnerving.

The evening marked a great beginning to the partnership between WWRL and The Dow Twins group (in fact, Marko Nobles first met his wife, Melissa, that night; and she later gave him *twins!*)

Embracing the dream of navigating and managing a New York City radio station in 1995 was a special chapter in my career journey. By 1997, the task at hand was to retool the station's iconic format from Gospel to an '80s/'90s urban music platform. This involved re-branding the station with a "Relive the Magic" theme and establishing strong, productive relationships within the music industry and with community partners to create events that would entice listeners and advertisers to support us. This is where The Dow Twins came in.

We partnered with them because they had a reputation as a focused, creative, and influential media company with more than twenty-five years of experience. Once they joined forces with WWRL-AM, we implemented a targeted marketing campaign to leverage the station's heritage and create excitement for the new format by crafting a series of headline-grabbing celebrity concerts and events titled the "Soul City Music Series."

I knew we had accomplished our mission when, on a cold evening in February 1998, I arrived at The Manhattan Center on Eighth Avenue and saw thousands of our listeners wrapped around the block. The Dow Twins delivered. It was pure joy! Over the years, Harold and Norman continued to embrace our dreams and "Relive the Magic" with many successful and memorable events hosted in partnership with the radio station. Our personal friendship will live forever.

❧

Adriane Gaines

To further market the radio station, we organized new summer outdoor activities at Chelsea Piers on 23rd Street, roller-skating and bowling outings, and cruises orchestrated by Marko. We also included WWRL's presence at our major events such as the USS Intrepid Gala, The Dow Twins' Scholarships Awards, and other notable activities in the New York market. It was a perfect partnership of two foremost New York influencers (WWRL and The Dow Twins) which lasted for twenty years, until 2018 when the station was sold.

My WWRL years fostered many happy memories. For example, 2011 was a special year when President Obama delivered a keynote address at the Reverend Al Sharpton's National Action Network (NAN) Convention in New York. Adriane and the Reverend were (and still are) good friends. In fact, the Reverend hosted his radio show, "Keep It Real," on WWRL. As a media partner, key personnel from the station were invited to attend President Obama's speech, including Rennie Bishop, Tony Morris, and me.

THE DOW TWINS' LEGACY

My friend, boss & mentor Adriane Gaines with Justice Vasquez

THE FORMULA FOR BRINGING PEOPLE TOGETHER

On the day of the speech, even though I was supposed to be credentialed, to Adriane's and my surprise my VIP pass was not at the security entrance when we arrived. Well, Adrienne wasn't having it. She said to security, "I personally sent all of our certifications in at the same time." Rather than hold things up, I told Adriane to go on in without me, but she wouldn't leave me until the mix-up was straightened out. That's what I loved about her. If you were on her team—broadcasting, sales, or anything—she would fight for you to the end. Great lady!

At one point, Adriane took Norman and I to check out the station's new Manhattan corporate offices (Syd Small moved the station's offices from Woodside to Seventh Avenue and 29th Street) across from the FIT—Fashion Institute of Technology—campus. While there, I noticed a gentleman who Norman and I used to pass on 35th Street near Justine's. He was always dressed in a suit, which caused us to notice and acknowledge him (even though we didn't know each other). Justine's neighborhood wasn't the safest in the 1970s or '80s and, because we didn't want to draw attention to ourselves, Norman and I often dressed very casually until we got inside the club—but we recognized a kindred spirit who appreciated wearing a nice suit.

To our surprise, the gentleman turned out to be Syd Small, the owner of WWRL. He knew exactly who we were, as we later found out, and he graciously welcomed me to the organization. Beyond this coincidence, Syd's son, Anthony, was a good friend of Norman's through his work with The Manhattan Proper Café, but neither of us had ever known who his father was. As they say, "it's a small world" out there; and Anthony remains a good friend even now.

WWRL 1600 owner Syd Small, accomplished jazz musicians and member of the Bartlett Contemporaries Carl Bartlett, WWRL GM Adriane Gaines, Devon Prioleau, Charles Pringle, Anissa Smith, Carlo Simpson, and successful author Tiffany Jackson at the 2000 Reginald N. Dow Memorial Scholars

Sometimes Syd would arrive at one of our WWRL events and just walk in, assuming that our door staff would know who he was. Luckily, I happened to be there the first time he did this, and I had to inform security that he owned the station (smile). Sadly, after only two events, Manhattan Center increased our rental fee and Syd agreed with us to cancel the remaining dates, even though our events there had been very successful up to that point. We then moved on to other venues that valued our business a bit more.

Syd was also very supportive of our activities, especially of our Dow Twins scholarships to high school graduating seniors. Sadly, Syd passed away in 2010. He is missed.

While most of the WWRL years were wonderful, there were dark times, too. For instance, I was at the Woodside offices on the morning of the devastating 9/11 attacks when the station got the news. We watched the two buildings collapse with all that gray smoke and debris, not realizing that the smoke was about to blow over to us in Queens and the surrounding area. The smell was awful and knowing that death and destruction were a part of that smell made it a truly terrible day for this lifelong New Yorker, as for so many others.

Upon learning details about the amount of devastation there was, Norman and I were concerned whether any of our friends, family or customers had been lost in the ruins of the World Trade Center (WTC). For years my brother and I had visited the WTC to promote our special events. We had walked around the plaza (which hosted free concerts in the summer) and talked to folks. We'd strolled along the same sidewalks where, in 2001, that massive cloud of gray smoke, fumes and 1.8 million tons of crashing building debris would destroy the neighborhood.

After the tragedy, I saw the faces of all the missing in photographs along the wall of Bellevue Hospital on First Avenue and 26th Street. Despite the enormity of loss, I only learned of one of our customers dying during 9/11, but I knew that there were many others.

In the aftermath of the attacks, I read stories in *The New York Times* about how the residents of Manhattan were afraid to leave their tiny New York apartments, which they had been trapped in for weeks. I again thought of our folks who, in addition to having cabin fever, hadn't been able to see their neighbors, train mates, club buddies, and co-workers, and didn't know who had survived the horrible Wall Street disaster.

With this in mind, Norman and I decided to host a reception near Thanksgiving just to get folks out and to give them a reason to celebrate life. It was held at a midtown club and was well-attended because people just wanted to see their friends, acquaintances, dance partners and the people they were used to seeing—*safe*! The reception became a lovefest with people hugging and embracing. The gathering, for some, was a positive mental health experience after such a devastating tragedy which we will never forget!

Tragically for me, 9/11 turned out not to be my most difficult time during my WWRL years. Four years later, in 2005, I lost my brother very suddenly and was devastated all over again.

Shortly after the funeral, I returned to the station and tried, with limited success, to handle business as usual. Adriane saw that I was struggling and said to me, "If you're having a moment, just close your office door and we'll understand." Of course, I told her this wasn't necessary, but before long I realized that it was. All it took was a statement, a song, or a photo to remind me of my brother, at which point tears would start flowing down my cheeks; or I wouldn't be able to finish a sentence involving Norman's name.

Fortunately, the WWRL team was very supportive of me during that stage of my life. In fact, soon after Norman's passing, a new WWRL sales manager, Tony Morris, recruited me fully onto the station's sales force, where I worked for eight more years. Over time, I was better able to handle my grief; and I will be forever grateful to everyone at WWRL.

THE FORMULA FOR BRINGING PEOPLE TOGETHER

Eddie Murphy and entourage at The Dow Twins' Red Parrot Affair

The U.S.S. Intrepid and Copacabana

In tandem with my tenure at WWRL, Norman and I continued to organize our "one-off" events at venues all over the city and beyond. Among these were mega-spaces such as the old and new Copacabana, the Red Parrot, the Palladium, Metronome, and the South Street Seaport. Our most celebrated and widely-attended special event location was our annual fêtes and benefits aboard the WWII aircraft carrier, the USS Intrepid Sea, Air & Space Museum, docked on the Hudson River in midtown Manhattan. Why this unusual location? Where do I begin …

Norman and I used to drive by the USS Intrepid all the time going uptown or downtown on the Westside Highway. One evening, we noticed the onboard lights illuminating the ship, which made it look spectacular against the night sky. We knew then that it would be a "hot" spot to give an event. I said to Norman, "Let's call our event agent, Marc Glazer. He knows everyone in NYC." Luckily for us, in 1985 (the year of our first Intrepid Gala), the ship wasn't booking many events; Mark knew the man in charge, so we were able to successfully negotiate for the space.

To make a long story short, our first event there was soon a done deal. Remembering the look on some my associates' faces when we invited them to participate in our plan to hold a party on a massive naval ship makes me smile even now. They were astonished.

> Norman and Harold had such loyal followers who loved what they did, but they outdid themselves this time. Who would ever have thought of having a party on an aircraft carrier?
>
>
>
> Justice Vasquez

Next, we had to decide how we were going to market the event, and who we should enlist to promote our new venture. We recruited key promoters—Harold DH (Stancil), Bob Belle and Fred Coleman from Philadelphia—and we had a lot of support from our own clients. We created a buzz in the market by announcing our plans to the thousands of folks on our database.

We marketed the event as an *"Adventure on the High Seas—An Unforgettable Evening with Live Entertainment and Dancing Under the Stars Aboard the Legendary Aircraft Carrier, the USS Intrepid."*

We hit every possible party and social gathering starting in the spring of 1985, spreading news of the event. Social media as we know it today wasn't in play then. There was no Twitter, Facebook, or even Email to get your message out to people back in the 1970s and '80s—only the US Postal Service and word of mouth. We had to use costly mailing—sending announcements to those on our personal database, and information sharing with our social influencers.

We focused on getting our message out, not to the public, but to our friends and their friends. This kept our event technically "private" and, thus, very manageable. Due to a limited budget and our preference for the "private party" approach, we decided not to pay for radio coverage with 107.5 WBLS—one of the most popular Black FM stations at the time. This decision surprised our salesman, Mark Neiman, but despite foregoing radio coverage, our other strategies worked like magic. Once people heard about the gala through the grapevine, the radio jocks and callers couldn't stop talking about it—so we got radio coverage anyway without having to pay for airtime.

The dream came true: legendary USS Intrepid hosting guests, The Hunts, with Norman Dow

Dancing on the deck of The USS Intrepid, 2009 Gala

The day of the event, Norman had the responsibility of "dressing" the ship for the evening's activities, including setting up chairs and tables on both decks and decorating the vast spaces with balloon clusters. He also tracked the weather report for the evening because some of the festivities would take place on an open deck.

THE FORMULA FOR BRINGING PEOPLE TOGETHER

His work and that of his team was spot-on by the time I arrived, after finalizing marketing for the grand occasion (I was always too nervous to be the first one on the ship). Now it was time for me to coordinate reserved seating, the DJ set-up, the live entertainment, and the arriving buses filled with out-of-towners revelers. Bus groups would call ahead with their ETAs, and I would leave the ship to oversee their arrival. This task, in later years, was assigned to one of our team leaders, with a minimum of eight buses bringing guests from Philadelphia and Boston.

Justice had her crew work the entrance with our only security man, Lawrence Darden. We were fortunate that security wasn't an issue. Most of our patrons were friends and acquaintances who didn't need any supervision; and others were just happy to be a part of this special night. Other team members, John Taylor, Harold Stancil, Bob Belle, and of course, Norman and I, hosted the evening and seated guests on board.

My name is Fred Coleman. I live in Philadelphia, Pennsylvania. I have known Harold for too many years to count. In Philly, I would promote social events and bus trips. So, one year I attended an event on the USS Intrepid hosted by The Dow Twins; I had such a great time I began hosting bus trips to New York (with six to seven busloads of people). We attended this unique event for twenty-three years; it opened a new demographic of Philadelphians for The Dow Twins. So many marriages were consummated as people from Philadelphia met people from New York and vice versa. Now Harold's reputation proceeds him in Philly because The Dow

Twins events were so awesome. Harold and I remain to be good friends to this day.

꙳

Fred Coleman
Co-producer of the USS Intrepid

In addition to the buses, lines of taxis and limousines pulled onto the pier from the West Side Highway, and folks dressed to the nines swelled at the entrance. Any number of celebrities, such as Melba Moore, Dorothy Height, WBLS's Ken "Spider" Webb, and Vaughn Harper joined in the fun. Ladies in their party dresses and high heels walked gingerly up the carrier's metal steps and into a thirty-foot high vaulted space to party the night away.

The ship was open to exploration. You could take a break from dancing and wander through the museum, which included everything from fighter jets hanging from the ceiling to glass cases filled with naval memorabilia. You could walk down the narrow passageways to the seamen's living quarters and galley, then back to the ballroom deck, where bartenders in white jackets served cocktails and folks packed the dance floor. Once the Latin band and the DJ on the lower hanger deck had concluded at 12:30 a.m., the finale was held upstairs on the flight deck under the stars. Normally, at least 1,500 folks of the initial 2,500-person crowd were still there after midnight to close out the party—dancing, romancing, mixing and mingling to the hottest sounds of our number-one New York City DJs Tommie Allen and Reggie Wells.

Manny Oquendo's Libre at the USS Intrepid Gala
with AA activist Dorothy Height & Melba Moore

After the inaugural year, the Intrepid gala became the "hottest ticket" in the tri-state area. Many lasting relationships and memories were created during the annual Intrepid event.

One classic memory was created at the end of the first gala in 1985. Not only was the event Sold Out, which kept us working at a fever pace all night long, but it had also been a super busy week for our team. We had just wrapped up one of the most incredible evenings in New York Black entertainment history.

Our Chevrolet & Moet Hennessy USA sponsors one year & the Raine Group UDV sponsors the next

After the long night, Norman and I relived the evening's highlights over an early morning breakfast before driving home to New Jersey. As soon as we arrived home, we got a call from the long shoremen's cleanup crew on the ship. They were phoning to inform us that they had found half a dozen folks in a restricted sleeping area on the lower levels of the ship! We were in disbelief that this had taken place on our watch, and our first reaction was to say, "Put them in the brig!" But the long shoreman just laughed and promised to send our guests on their way. We later found out that some guests had been taking advantage of an impromptu "make out" area near the bridge to the outside deck that faced 42nd Street.

This hiccup aside, thereafter we were able to give events or private invitational parties wherever we wanted, due to our (near) pristine record.

Another year, during the Intrepid gala, we noticed a gentleman on the pier moving quickly towards the ship carrying an enormous cooler. Justice, Norman, and I watched with curious anticipation, wondering if he was on the wrong pier or something. As he approached the reception desk, we inquired as to

THE FORMULA FOR BRINGING PEOPLE TOGETHER

where he was going and what he was looking for. His breathless response was, "Did I miss the boat?"

A bit taken aback, we answered, "No, and this isn't a boat ride. This is an aircraft carrier, and it isn't going anywhere." It was only when he saw the quizzical looks on our faces that he finally looked up at the ship and realized his error. He was so embarrassed. He was clearly late for some other boat and already very distressed. It was all we could do not to laugh out loud as he rushed off to find the right pier. But, as soon as he was out of earshot, we exploded into laughter.

Our Intrepid run lasted so long that an intergenerational group of clients attended over time—young folks, their parents, and their parents! Among these were Cheryl Fenton, whose grandfather attended with her, and Gladys Stallings, whose son attended the Intrepid parties with her when he was old enough. These are their memories:

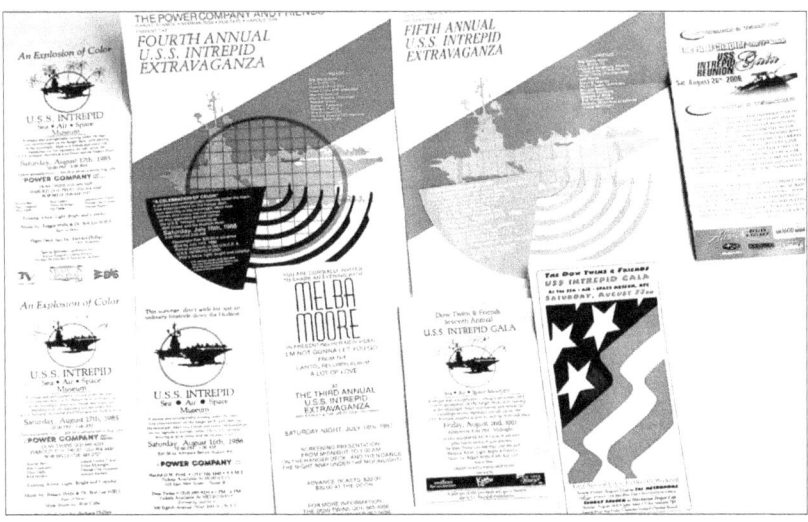

Norman and I hosted 2,500 people annually on the Intrepid for twenty-five years, from 1985 – 2010!

Harold awarding prizes for 'Best Nautical Outfits'

"The Last Man Standing"

Before getting up this morning, I found myself thinking about my grandfather—a feisty West Indian soul who liked his Appleton rum punches, politics, people younger than himself and, I must say, women.

One year in August, I decided to celebrate my birthday during one of The Dow Twins' events on the USS Intrepid. I invited about ten or so of my closest girlfriends and decided to invite my grandfather to hang out with us young girls.

He was so excited, and very impressed at how these two Black guys were able to host such a huge event on a famous ship. This made it memorable for him. In addition, the huge attendance of good-looking people of color—and women—put the icing on the cake. Excited he was.

If you really think about it, a venue like that during those early years was very impressive.

THE FORMULA FOR BRINGING PEOPLE TOGETHER

What a fun time I had seeing my grandfather dancing all night with my friends and other women on the ship. He even bought drinks for us. All night he just kept us laughing and dancing.

At the end of the night, it was announced that Leviticus would be open if anyone wanted to continue partying. I was on my last leg, but a couple of us (including grandfather) decided to drive over to Leviticus. Once again, we were all dancing and laughing until, one by one, my girlfriends started dropping to the sidelines. But grandfather was still going strong.

I asked, "How can you still be dancing?"

He said, "I don't do anything fancy, and I stick to the same step!"

Well, I was tired, so I sat down to rest.

Before I knew it, my grandfather had disappeared, so I went looking for him. I found him asking a couple of guys if he could get coffee. I told him that they didn't serve coffee at Leviticus and asked him why he needed coffee when we could just go home. He said the coffee wasn't for him. He wanted to buy coffee for the girls. They were knocked out!

Yes, I have to say my grandfather, who was more than thirty years older than we were, was the last man standing that night.

This is a simple story, but to me it was one of my best birthdays because it just made me so happy to see my grandfather have so much fun. This probably—no—I know this <u>would</u> not have happened if it were not for Harold and Norman.

Grandfather passed away a long time ago, but the memories I have of that night are still fresh in my mind. To this day, my friends today still talk about that night.

Cheryl Fenton
Long-time supporter

I met Norman and Harold many, many years ago when they began their journey to have the best social events. Their events created a high level of meeting and greeting for professional individuals with wonderful careers and interesting jobs. A Dow party was a fun time—no fights, arguments or confusion. We looked forward to the next event as soon as the current one ended. Socialization was very healthy for our physical and mental states.

Many venues were utilized. The Intrepid was one of my favorites. Leviticus, The Copa, The Red Parrot, and many other venues. Memories will last a lifetime.

Gladys Q. Stallings
Long-time supporter

Other highlights of the gala were the door prizes, raffles, and contests. We awarded prizes for "Best Nautical Outfit" and "Best White on White Outfits" and gave away luxury mini vacations. One was given to Mickie Mullings:

THE FORMULA FOR BRINGING PEOPLE TOGETHER

One of my fondest Dow Twins memories began on the iconic USS Intrepid ship. It was unheard of for an African American promoter group to host an event in such a prestigious New York City venue. The Dow Twins rented the entire ship. Harold said the event was sold out and he expected 2,500 guests.

It was a beautiful summer evening on July 16th, 1986. Most of us wore white. Some wore sailor-inspired attire. The vibe was elegant, festive and glamorous.

The Dow Twins partnered with DeKuyper Peachtree Schnapps to promote its beverage product. While we were there, Harold and Norman enlisted the help of "The Dow Twins' Cuties," aka Charlie's Angels—which was Nelly Brathwaite, Millie Parrilla and me (nicknamed Mickie). We pinch hit as bartenders, and long lines ensued. Harold reported that the beverage sales revenue skyrocketed at the extravaganza, thanks to his lady bartenders. The guests loved our sales pitches and wanted to taste any beverage we were selling!

Some folks danced to the hottest DJs at the time—Reggie Wells and Tommie Allen. Some toured the ship. Some strolled the outside on the deck. It was a great event.

A few hours into the party, a raffle was scheduled to take place with assorted prizes. The grand prize was a trip to Martha's Vineyard with John Harley of the famous Tuskegee Airmen. Many of us purchased raffle tickets to support The Dow Twins. At the appointed time,

Norman and Harold had several ticket sellers pull the winning raffle tickets. When it got to the grand prize, guess whose number was called? Mine! I won the trip to Martha's Vineyard. I think some folks thought it was a fix because they knew I was close to Harold and Norman. But I didn't know the folks pulling the winning tickets and it was not a fix.

We decided on a mutually beneficial date for Harold, John Harley and me to fly up to the Vineyard for the day. I invited my cousin Dickie Orridge because I thought he'd enjoy the trip and would be a great complement to the group. We had a picture-perfect day to fly. It was after the Martha's Vineyard high season, and what a pleasure it was to not have to drive to the ferry, but to take a short plane ride instead. We had the best time getting to know each other. The group commented that my cousin Dickie could talk! I smiled— "Yes he can!" The trip was so exciting. When we arrived on the island, we had a leisurely lunch and walked around the Vineyard. I had not been there in years. John Harley was a regular on Martha's Vineyard and helped us navigate the island. After a time, he realized it was getting late, so he recommended that we stay overnight. Oh my! I didn't pack any clothes! Maybe the only one who packed was the pilot. So, I purchased a few items, and our group found an inn to rent rooms for the night.

After dinner and more fantastic conversation we finally went to bed. The next day, we had breakfast and John recommended we head out. As we drove to the airport, John asked if we were up to flying to Sag Harbor. The response was a collective and resounding, "Yes! Let's do this!"

We left Martha's Vineyard and flew to Sag Harbor. Clear blue skies and more great conversation, including John's stories of his flight experiences. When we landed, we had lunch and a stroll around the town. We then flew to Teterboro Airport, where we landed and said very reluctant goodbyes.

That was a whirlwind weekend that capped an iconic event on the Intrepid. I am grateful to The Dow Twins for many of my fondest, most spontaneous life adventures.

Thank you, Dow Twins—Harold, Norman and all of the partners—for enriching my life with spontaneity and pure fun!

૭

Michele (Mickie) Mullings
Friend and supporter

USS Intrepid Host: Norman, Harold, Harold DH and Bob Belle

The DeKuyper Times   "What drinks these liqueurs make!"

The Power Company Powers DeKuyper

Oct 1986   New York Nightclub's Fund Raiser aboard U.S.S. Intrepid Brings Out 3,000 Party Goers...and New Fans for DeKuyper Peachtree Schnapps.

The Power Company owns and operates four outstanding nightclubs and a bar in New York City. During their 25 years in the nightclub business, the management team has built up a following of more than 10,000 people who participate in various promotional ventures conducted by the company, usually fundraisers in support of community programs. One recent event was a disco aboard the "floating museum," the U.S.S. Intrepid, tied up at a Manhattan dock. The party hosted more than 3,000 people.

Peachtree Sails Along

At the party, which benefitted the U.S.S. Intrepid Foundation and The United Negro College Fund, DeKuyper Peachtree Schnapps was prominently showcased. Signs promoting the drink were posted conspicuously, and John Harley, National Distillers sales representative, arranged to have an unusual raffle...a private aircraft trip for two to Martha's Vineyard in Massachusetts for a day was the prize.

The winner of the raffle was Michele Mullings, Ms. Mullings, her friend Ellen Edwards, Distributor salesman Ron Scoon and Harold Dow, who represented The Power Company, all made the one-day trip to the Island, whose pilot was none other than John Harley.

The Big Apple Has Gone Peaches aboard the U.S.S. Intrepid.

1986 USS Intrepid sponsor: DeKuyper PEACHTREE Schnapps

Every year, Intrepid attendance surpassed the record from the previous year (although no one at the Intrepid Museum ever thanked us or even acknowledged our sizeable annual contributions to the Museum Foundation). Because the event consistently met standards of quality, it established precedence for, and commanded, a higher level of local and national business support, participation and sponsorship, such as the DeKuyper Peachtree Schnapps sponsorship. The more high-profile the annual gala became, the more sponsorship funds we could command, which ultimately served to keep the price of admission reasonable for our clientele.

We developed a real history of dealing with sponsors, starting with DeKuyper and continuing with different liquor companies throughout the years. At the time, many of these companies were independent, and we had to be creative to make deals that satisfied each. The price of the sponsorship had a lot to do with the number of guests our event was projected to have. Norman and I always under-projected our guest turnout numbers, so when we exceeded expectations, our sponsors would celebrate and feel good about their decision to support us. This is one of the reasons so many sponsors remained with us for so long—we always delivered the number of patrons we promised.

In the early years, Norman and I were inexperienced with sponsors and didn't know how much of a fee to charge. We felt fortunate to have any sponsors at all. But eventually we met Lorraine Caldwell, a serious event marketer just starting her own agency, "B12," which designed marketing strategies for major events nationwide. Looking to expand her client base with some Black businesses, she met me at the annual Black Enterprise Entrepreneur's Summit, where I was able to introduce her to some of the folks I knew. When she learned how little we were getting from sponsors, she schooled us immediately and explained that, given the audience size, quality, and upscale venues that were hallmarks of our parties, we could ask for—and would get—many times more than we'd been receiving. And she was right!

> It was my good fortune to meet The Dow Twins at an after-work networking event in 1995. I do not remember the location of the event or the date and time, but what I do remember is that I was deeply impressed with the professional quality of the event and with The Dow Twins, who were possibly the best NYC event promoters. Each of their events that I attended that year was consistently very well organized, the food was good, the music was awesome, and the following was professional African

Americans. As a single woman attending with a girlfriend, we never felt unsafe or intimidated by the crowd. Their events felt like family, although there were several hundred people in attendance.

At that time, I had just moved from Connecticut to New Jersey for a position as a marketing manager for an international beverage company that did not promote their products to the African American community. Over time, I got to know Harold and Norman and learned about some of their unique marketing opportunities with the African American consumer. I had never worked with or marketed any products to my own people, and I knew very little about how to approach them. The Twins played a major role in my development with the information and knowledge that I learned through extensive conversations with Harold and Norman.

In 2000, I was offered the opportunity to start my own ethnic promotional marketing and events agency, The Raine Group LLC. My first client was an international beverage company. I was given the challenge to promote Smirnoff Vodka, Baileys Irish Cream, Jose Cuervo Tequila, Crown Royal and Captain Morgan Rum to the African American market in the Northeast region. Harold Dow was the first person that I called to arrange for sponsorship of several Dow Twins' events.

From that time on, we partnered in many events in the NYC market, along with National Brotherhood of Skiers events at resorts throughout the country and Canada. We went directly to very upscale resorts such as Vail, Copper

Mountain and Keystone, Colorado; Park City, Utah; and Whistler in Canada. With each event our reach increased, and the money spent by the brands that I managed grew with each successful year.

Because of the open relationship shared, we experienced a new level of partnering and I was in a position to sponsor many of The Dow Twins' events. I can remember encouraging Harold to ask for more dollars for their events from their other sponsors, such as actual payback dollars. As I look back, I do not know if any of us really capitalized on the real value that The Dow Twins and The Raine Group offered our clients at that time. We were just grateful for the business. The Twins had a very professional, high-income following that traveled for miles to their events, and money was no object because they realized the value that The Twins were giving them. A very good, memorable time.

༄

Lorraine Caldwell
Corporate sponsor

Our most successful sponsor relationship was with the Kobrand Corporation out of France, which was trying to market a new liqueur made of their finest cognac and passion fruit, called *"Alize."* The promotion started at about the time of our first Intrepid gala. Kobrand wanted us to give *Alize* away for free to our customers, but we couldn't agree to that because of our monetary commitment to the bar. What we could do was offer the drink at a discount. Kobrand agreed; and anyone who purchased three drinks received a beautiful, full-color *Alize* t-shirt.

Alize, first introduced to the world on The USS Intrepid Museum affair

Not surprisingly, *Alize* was sampled by many at the event and every available case was sold. It was especially popular with the ladies, and it had quite a kick to it, as some of them soon found out (smile).

Our client was thrilled, to say the least. Unfortunately, it took another three months to ship more product from France. Meanwhile, our guests began asking for *Alize* at their local retail liquor stores, which, in turn, were begging for deliveries of the new liqueur that had been sold on the USS Intrepid. The *Alize* launch was more successful than Kobrand Corporation could ever have hoped for, and they rewarded us by sponsoring more of our events throughout the city and across the country, including some with the National Black Skiers (NBS), WWRL radio, and our annual scholarship awards ceremony. They even went on to sponsor some of our competitors. All in all, the relationship resulted in a positive outcome for all concerned.

Alize promotion at The Copa and NBS gathering

Another memorable venue during our "roving party" years was The Copacabana at its initial location at 10 East 60th Street, and at its subsequent sites on the Westside Highway at 34th Street near the Javits Center and on 48th Street in the Theater

District. No matter which location, The Copa was always a popular favorite with our followers. We already had a relationship with Copa owner, John Juliano, who opened Pippin's club in the 1970s—a venue that Norman and I had booked in the past. The Copa events went so well that we became fast friends and hosted numerous parties at the club's various locations, especially the gorgeous 34th Street venue (this was the same location where my twin brother, Norman, first became ill and was rushed to the hospital before passing away just seven days later. John was physically sickened by this, after such a long history of doing business with us).

Once, an event we hosted at the Copa became so crowded that the police tried to shut us down:

> One night, the NYPD tried to close the club at 2:00 a.m. due to overcrowding. My son Steven was running the club that night and asked me what he should do. He didn't want to have to return everyone's money. I thought of a strategy and told him, "With a thousand people inside, you can't just close abruptly. So, tell the officers that we'll close slowly so as not to create a panic in the coatroom." That gave us extra time.
>
> Meanwhile, in lieu of refunds, we offered everyone a "rainy day" coupon to return at their convenience. I later asked Steven how many passes were used. He said, "Maybe one hundred were used out of the 1,000 we gave away." Wow! We had averted a financial disaster.

John Juliano
Owner of Silver Shadow, Pippin's, Bentley's and The Copacabana

THE FORMULA FOR BRINGING PEOPLE TOGETHER

The Copa served as a venue for our spring MASKquerade parties, for the Justine's / Leviticus / Red Parrot Reunion affairs, and even for an event we hosted in honor of the club's exclusive Opening Night, with a sit-down dinner at the 34th Street location.

Our final event was held in 2018 as a Christmas Celebration, at the 48th Street and Eighth Avenue location. The holiday spirit was tremendous and joyous. The eventual closing of the Copacabana was a terrible loss for our community and for the historic club's loyal fans, including many from Canada and Mexico. We did not yet realize that the pandemic was on its way.

Our success during these years was propelled by marketing and promotions. Norman and I understood from our marketing classes at St. John's University that promotions and creativity were essential to long-lasting profitability. To address creativity, we created one-off party events at dozens of venues all over NYC. Some of NYC's favorite spots were the Groove Factory, Gatsby's, the Prince George Hotel, Colony, Cork and Bottle, The Late Show, Le Cocu, Nemo's Hideaway, Headrest, Sweetwater's, Jimmy's, Iron Horse, Adrian's, Act 1, La Martinique, Alexander the Great, Le Joint, Pippin's, Spindletop, Casablanca, Corso, Red Parrot, Charles Gallery, Barney Googles, The Cheetah, and The Ginza.

I would be remiss not to say that, regarding our promotions strategy, "we stood on the shoulders" of the very best in the business including Russell Cress, 3+1, SOB's, Now Generation, Kenny Floyd, Harris and Lindsay, Bob Cagle, Elmo, Top Shelf, Nat and Ray, The Smith Bros., Winston, We Four Guys, Jet Procter, Dee King and Cathy Barbee, Vanilla Fudge, Jerry Roebuck, Gene Smith, Harold Maynard and assistants Hubie, Willie Dee, Elbert T., Ferguson and LD.

Equally vital to our success story were our DJs: Pete 'DJ' Jones, Larry D., Ron Plummer, Derrick Gaines, Reggie Wells. Johnny Allen, Richard Hot, Rip and Cliff, Thomas Pearson, Bucky Wynn, Gary Brodus, Bert Morgan, Flowers, KC and Carl TNT, Tommie Allen and Lady DJ Wells. We owe you *all* a debt of gratitude.

Many fashionable masks at our annual MASKqueade events

THE FORMULA FOR BRINGING PEOPLE TOGETHER

Great People image

CHAPTER FOUR

Giving People a Reason to Be Cheerful

Late 1980s and 1990s Hit Songs

"How Do You Keep the Music Playing" by Tito Nieves
"If I Could" by Regina Belle
"No Scrubs" by TLC

The Dow Twins' 20th Anniversary Gala

In 1989, after providing social activities at high-end venues all over the city and beyond, the time had come to step up our game and host a black tie event. My brother and I had been in business for twenty years, and we agreed that we should use the occasion to celebrate our two-decade adventure.

As the location for our anniversary gala, we chose one of the most elite and famous hotels in New York City—the historic Waldorf Astoria. Like the Intrepid, at that time the Waldorf Astoria was rarely chosen as an event site by Black party promoters, and the hotel was skeptical when Norman and I assured them that we could fill the grand ballroom with 800 guests at $100 per ticket. Hotel management asked our dinner coordinator, Randreta Ward-Evans, "Who are these gentlemen? Can they really attract that many young adults to a formal dinner gala?" Of course we could, and we did.

Even though the price of the venue was exorbitant, we chose not to pass this cost on to our guests. We only charged enough to break even. It was important to us to keep this and all our events affordable for our loyal followers. That being said, for our clientele cost was never really a problem as long as the event was unique enough.

We were informed by Waldorf management that a certain number of advance tickets sales was essential to secure hotel catering. Our pre-event count, however, was only half the number required; but we knew our folks tended to be a little late committing. The Waldorf representative decided that it would not be a problem since so many of our guests had made weekend room reservations; the hotel would not cancel our event under these circumstances. That information was a welcome stress reliever for us, and we were on the road to a sold-out gala night.

When the date finally arrived, the only problem left to face was how to arrange the seating plan without offending any of our many friends and colleagues. We had business partners, preferred friends, sponsors and personal friends. We also had to ensure that each table had ten guests while dealing with the occasional group that had an odd number of nine or eleven. Thank goodness for our dinner coordinator, who helped us resolve most of these problems.

The evening's guests came from our college days, from new associates, from business relationships, and from family and friends who were just plain proud to help us celebrate two decades of entrepreneurial spirit. The evening was joyous and sophisticated. The ladies were elegant in their evening gowns, as were the gentlemen in their tuxedos, which gave the grand ballroom an atmosphere that some of our folks had not seen since their cotillion days. Our photographer, Gerald Peart, did a great job capturing guests naturally in conversation and dancing; he also took more formal shots to memorialize the evening.

Food and champagne flowed, and music filled the room. Before dinner, the evening benediction prayer was administrated by Dr. Calvin O. Butts from Abyssinian Baptist Church. Recorded video messages of congratulations played on a jumbotron screen. These came from our many celebrity friends and acquaintances, including actor Paul Newman and then-mayor Ed Koch.

Remy Amerique's Andy Glover, Guest & 20th Anniversary Dinner Coordinator Randreta Ward-Evans

THE DOW TWINS' LEGACY

Harold Dow, Rev. Calvin Butts, Norman Dow & Dr. Anita Underwood

Folks at The Dow Twins' Waldorf Astoria, 1989

Norman just liked to have fun, and he loved women. I knew every female Norman dated and became best friends with many of his exes. If I didn't like someone, they didn't make the cut. Once, he said to me after going through his calendar and seeing how many women's names were there, "I think I'm a ho'!"

I answered sarcastically, "Are you just finding that out?" Then I smiled and said, "We'll keep it out little secret."

Harold Stancil brought men to The Twins' parties, but Harold and Norman brought the women.

೬

Justice Vasquez

We took the opportunity to incorporate a fundraising element into the festivities to honor our dad—the Inaugural Reginald N. Dow Memorial Fundraiser. It was a perfect chance, we thought, to acknowledge the generosity of our clientele and sponsors whose donations and ticket purchases were used to create financial scholarships for qualified high school students preparing to graduate.

The funds raised went to the United Negro College Fund to support two incoming St. John's University freshman. Any child of our patrons was eligible to apply. The selection committee was chaired by scholar Dr. Anita Underwood, and awards were presented the night of the gala to the deserving students. What a night! And all this for a price that some professionals in the business thought was beyond the reach of our vast circle of followers.

But The Dow Twins' folks did not disappoint. They rallied around us and eagerly opened their purses and wallets for a gold plate dinner and scholarship awards, all with dancing and laughter.

Mr.& Mrs. Chris Gunzel (standing) with Mr. & Mrs. Bill Woods (seated)

WBLS Vaughn Harper, Joe Sanbria, Tony Blades,
Norman & Harold Dow, G. Keith Alexander

GIVING PEOPLE A REASON TO BE CHEERFUL

Wes Powell, Harold Dow, Bob Cagle & Norman Dow with their wives

Kathyll Carnegie, her mom, Harold Dow and friends

On the dais: WBLS The Quiet Storm's Vaughn Harper with CNN Cheryl Washington and CD 101.9 Pat Prescott

Kenneth Black, Mr. & Mrs. Jacques Shepherd, Harold Dow & Oscar Sing Jr

GIVING PEOPLE A REASON TO BE CHEERFUL

The re-imagination of our evening's program cover by Gloria Lockett

Norman Dow, James Walker, Kathyll Carnegie, Evelyn Dow, Harold Dow, Dawne Steward, Vaughn Harper and Steve Roberts. Photo: Gerald Peart

The Formula for Long-Term Success

Acutely aware of the impending challenges we faced in our quest to sustain a captive audience as we moved into the last decade of the 20th century, Norman and I decided to expand the notion of only specializing in a regional market. We knew that our longevity in the field of special events development and management required a more aggressive and nationally-focused business plan. The 1990s saw an expansion of our activities and a new mantra: "Giving people a reason to be cheerful." The theme served as an ideal antidote for the angst of a decade that would end, unspeakably, in the 9/11 attacks.

Norman and I had long since been traveling extensively, and we met people wherever we went. In addition to our many other life experiences, travel helped us to develop well-rounded personalities. We understood that personality traits such as charm, respect for others, genuine warmth, and a great smile were important to our professional success and to making our people happy—which was our ultimate goal.

> There is a resistance movement today for "Reclaiming Black Joy"—as an antidote to racism, police shootings and inequity of all kinds. As a racial justice theme, Black Joy is something that The Dow Twins understood decades ago. Joy abounded at their parties, which catered to Black and brown communities getting together and doing their thing. The music, the camaraderie, seeing the same wonderful people at each event—all of these things made you joyous.
>
> The Dow Twins events welcomed all different kinds of people without judgement. One night, arriving at

Manhattan Proper, I ran into the mother of my next-door neighbors from my childhood in Jamaica, Queens. Her name was Mrs. Whitley, and she was in her eighties hanging out at Manhattan Proper with her new boyfriend!

The Twins welcomed everyone. Their events were among the few that I could attend and feel completely at ease and know that no one would care what race I was. Race often was (and still is) an issue for me in social and professional situations because I am bi-racial and look white, even though I grew up in a Black neighborhood. The Dow Twins (and their community) didn't care. Whenever they saw me and my sisters, Harold and Norman would exclaim, "The Farrington sisters are here!" I got a personal feeling of freedom and knew that I could get my party on without any judgement. It was like visiting family.

In fact, lots of people attended Dow events with their kids—myself included. Our white mom (sadly deceased in 1996) and her Black boyfriend hung out at Manhattan Proper, too. I remember their favorite spot at the bar there. My sister Lisa gave her thirty-fifth and fortieth birthday parties at Dow venues—Club Broadway and Metronome. Her friends—African American, German, Chinese—all came to her parties, along with our parents, and danced the night away with carefree abandon. Our mom and dad, then in their sixties, even joined the "Soul Train" line!

Once while I was a medical resident, I escaped from arduous and stressful hours at Queens Hospital Center (a typically over-extended and under-funded city hospital at the time) and went to an Intrepid party. I danced until 2:00 or 3:00

a.m., even though I knew I had to go back to the hospital in a few hours. The Intrepid gala was stress relief for me because I knew that I could dance all night, release my tension, and be better able to deal with the traumas of my job.

The bigger picture is what The Dow Twins meant to the Black community. They provided spiritual sustenance and healing in a safe environment where you could feel the fullness of your personhood—where you mattered.

Leslie Farrington, MD

Lisa, mom & friends partying with The Twins

Salsa Fridays at Club Broadway with staff, Norman, John Taylor and Harold

Norman, in particular, knew how to make people smile. He could talk to men and women alike, putting them at ease or building their confidence. He was the perfect host. At any one of our events, Norman could always be found trouble-shooting challenges at the door with Justice and team member John Taylor. You know how folks are: "I lost my ticket," "I left my ticket at home," "Could you find my friend inside?" "Are you going to play salsa tonight?!" and a multitude of other questions and concerns. And he constantly had a smile on his face. While I was looking through photos after his death in 2005, I was hard-pressed to find one where he wasn't smiling. Everyone could always count on receiving a big hug, smile or strong handshake from him upon entering one of our many venues.

He was also a good listener. If you came to him with a problem or question, he always offered a helpful opinion. He was willing to listen, review and suggest a meaningful remedy for any concern that was brought to him.

Whenever Norman found himself at the front door of an event greeting the patrons coming in, he was irresistible, especially to the ladies. Harold and I had a saying, "Norman could turn a hug into a meal!" Everyone loved to hug Norman! Could it have been his cologne? I'm sure he's one of the greeters at the gates of heaven! In Denzel's voice, "My Man!"

Ray James
Long-time friend

I, on the other hand, had different talents. I was never as instinctively charming and cheerful as Norman, but I had a real head for business and made sure that things ran smoothly. I always saw my role as keeping Norman happy. He had to be "on" all the time—always upbeat and welcoming—to keep our customers coming back. I felt that he didn't need to be burdened with the other side of the business; that was my job.

Although some may have found me distant because I didn't have Norman's outgoing demeanor, the comparison seemed unreasonable, to say the least. Despite our physical likeness, we had never been the same person. While Norman was very trusting of the people we met, I wasn't as easily swayed. Although we both believed that trust in business and friendships should be an integral part of any relationship (otherwise what's the point), I knew, intuitively, that people weren't always what they seemed. I was more aware than Norman that others might be envious of the attention we received, of what we had, or of how we were held in high regard by so many folks.

I guess it's the old "crabs in the barrel" mentality. Even though we were raised to be trusting and to always support and uplift our friends, not everyone appreciated our desire to be helpful. Some saw this as a weakness and an excuse to take advantage of us. Believe me, even with my cautious nature, I've been fooled more times than I would like to admit.

Needless to say, I was always my own man, and I hoped that people would accept that rather than judge it. In my role as the pragmatic and dedicated businessman, I was good at scouting out new venues, designing flyers, handling finances, and supervising the behind-the-scenes activities for The Dow Twins' brand. I also created and maintained our database, which reached 50,000 people at its peak (pre-Facebook!), and kept our followers aware of activities by way of our brochure mailings "City Lights" and "Sneak Preview."

I also continued to develop our relationships with sponsors. In dealings with various beverage companies, we were able to produce new high-end events and maintain reasonable cost for loyal patrons, like Doreen Johnson says:

The Dow Twins' events were parties that no one ever wanted to miss; and if you did miss a Dow event, you heard about it the next day and were disappointed that you weren't there. Their parties were like celebrity gatherings that everyone looked forward to. My friends and I were not celebrities, but The Twins made everyone feel special, as if we had celebrity status and belonged among the real celebrities that were present.

I always had lots of fun, and I loved to dance to the great music that the famous DJs played. The music was always great, and I danced to just about every song played. All their parties were gathering places where you could see special friends, dance with special partners, and meet new friends.

There was always someone celebrating their birthday with a big cake and lots of special guests. I remember my girlfriend Valerie's birthday at a Dow party. It was a very special evening. Her cake was beautiful, and she had all of her friends to help her celebrate.

Everyone was dressed to impress, whether it was a nighttime or afterwork party. Harold often wore a suit with a white dress shirt, and he walked around the dance hall making sure everything was going the way it was supposed to.

One of my favorite memories is of Norman, who was usually up front near the entrance greeting everyone coming in. Norman always gave big hugs, and I loved it. So, every time I came in, I would fall into his arms and get the biggest hug ever! I can still feel his hug today. It was that special. If I came in and Norman was busy with other guests, I would stand there and wait my turn until he was free for my big hello and hug. I always wanted The Twins to know I was there.

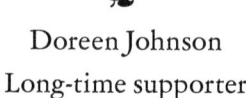

Doreen Johnson
Long-time supporter

An important characteristic that Norman and I shared was human observation. We were always observing people because we were fascinated by the types of activities and experiences that made people happy.

We especially used our travel adventures to seek out new concepts for entertainment back home (our good buddy, Vincent Scott from St. Catherine's Elementary School, was the first to encourage us to go sightseeing in Europe). Watching what people enjoyed abroad gave us insight into what our New York City clientele might like. We people-watched in the great museums of the UK; we spent time in the many clubs in Acapulco and Mexico; and we made note of the most popular culinary trends at the ski resorts we visited in various European countries.

Harold, Norman and friends at their "Happy Place" in Acapulco, Mexico, late '70s

One of our annual people-watching activities was the New York City Marathon, which attracted throngs of well-wishers from around the world in addition to marathon participants. We could see that athletic events really drew people together, and we always supported our friends in their athletic endeavors.

On NYC Marathon Sunday, you could always find The Twins at their regular spot on First Avenue in Spanish Harlem. They would patiently wait for me and the other seven-minute mile runners. Of course, sometimes I was slower than I wanted to be, but they always waited for me and had sports drinks and oranges to help me through the Harlem leg of the run. Then they would jog over and meet me in Central Park at the finish line.

Ray James

We capitalized on our insights to create new and exciting themed events which, in addition to parties, involved awards nights, travel excursions, and sports—particularly skiing.

Our reimagined strategy worked like a charm to keep our home audience engaged. For instance, we instituted the "Summer Finale"—an afterwork party to mark the end of the summer. The multi-activity fête started at 6:00 p.m. and ended at 4:00 a.m. and only required one entrance fee—something unheard of back in the day.

Another idea involved the creation of a high-end corporate type of event—so, the "Prestige 100 Awards" were conceived to acknowledge our five-star patrons for whom we organized many exclusive affairs, including Hudson River boat rides, Broadway play nights, Carnival in Rio, Black Tie Galas and Norman's idea to honor the World Champion New York Knicks with a cocktail reception at Leviticus. We also hosted a women's-only male stripper night there, which was a big hit.

One year after I saw an episode of "The Jefferson's" where "Weezy" goes to a male strip show, I scouted out where I might see such a show myself and, of course, The Dow Twins were ahead of the curve. They had organized an afterwork male strip show at Leviticus. I remember going by myself and sitting down front with all the excited ladies. Out came the stripper! Nearly naked, gyrating and coming up to each lady one by one. The crowd went wild.

Everyone but me, that is. My Catholic schoolgirl upbringing had not prepared me to see a naked man in public and, much to my own surprise, I was truly embarrassed. I didn't want to look stupid, so I discreetly removed myself to the bar, far away from the stage. Next thing I knew, Norman was standing at my shoulder. He figured out that I was "chicken" and said, grinning, "If you don't get back down there to the stage, I'm gonna make the dancer come to you!"

I was horrified at the prospect, but Norman had only been teasing. He laughed and let me stay in my corner, watching the spectacle from a safe distance. This was my first Dow Twins experience, but it would not be my last—not by about forty years.

❧

Lisa Farrington
Loyal friend and supporter

We also hosted an "Excellence and Achievement in Entertainment Salute" to singer-songwriter Stephanie Mills, whose album *Home* had gone gold in 1989 – 1990 (Stephanie was a friend of Ray James, who introduced us to her in the early years at Justine's, when we'd arranged for Stephanie to test out a couple of her new tracks at the club). For the "Excellence" ceremony we chose a Thursday afterwork night, which was a popular party night.

Stephanie was surprised at the crowd's enthusiastic response to her disco-style soundtracks. She modestly thought that people were just being supportive because she was there in person. She couldn't have been more wrong. Those tracks and more all went gold that year, along with one of her earliest R&B albums, *What Cha Gonna Do with My Lovin'*. At the ceremony, Stephanie presented Norman and I with one of her gold albums, which we were very honored to receive.

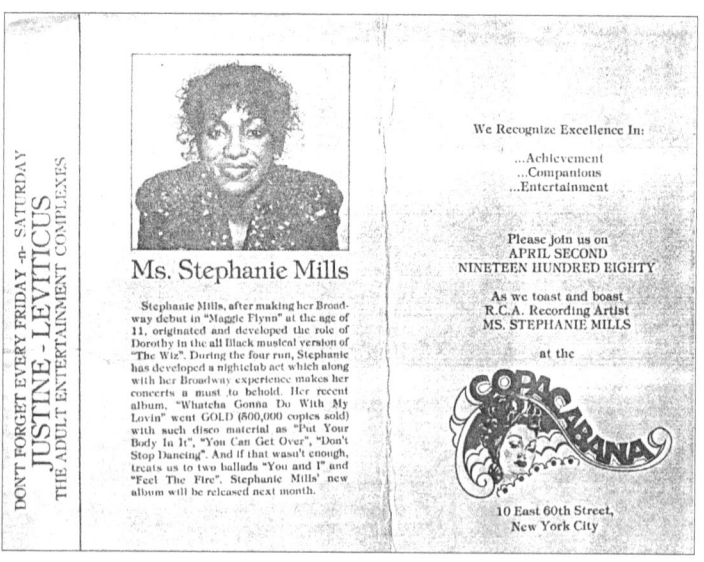

Stephanie Mills honored

So Many Reasons to Be Cheerful

Other Dow Twins "reasons to be cheerful" events included trips to Atlanta, Bear Mountain, and Belmont Racetrack, which our supporters remember fondly.

Norman and Harold always had events that everyone enjoyed. I remember one summer they had a bus ride to Bear Mountain. The bus ride was entertaining, going and coming. When we got to the park, some of us went over to the lake and some went to the pool.

Later in the day, a bunch of the guys were on the lawn relaxing in the hot summer sun when the girls ran out from the picnic area with balloons and garbage bags filled with water. They threw water on all of us. Well, we all started chasing them, throwing water balloons back at them. It broke up into laughter and people coupling off. Later that evening we all ended up at a backyard party.

Garth Ramsey
Childhood friend

During this period, I was very blessed to have the love and support of many friends who stepped into the empty space that Norman had always occupied in my life. One such friend, Charlie Davis, was always asking if I wanted to attend a NY Nets games or go to the CIAA (Central Intercollegiate Athletic Association) basketball tournament in Charlotte, NC. Having said "no" a few times, I finally agreed to hang out with his Boys High alumni crew between 2015 and 2018.

Our mother, Evelyn S. Dow & friends started "The Day at the Races" at Belmont Racetrack. Norman & I continued the series over thirty years of beautiful hats and smiles

Our Sno-burners' Ski Club turnout at Belmont Racetrack for our annual Father's Day

The guys took me in, even though I was about four years younger. Their conversations and fellowships were just what I needed. They had me laughing, drinking (just a little) and their recollections of mischief-making at previous CIAA reunions were mind-blowing (and fun) to hear. We had such a good time together that most of us never got to the actual basketball games. Many thanks to the Boys High crew and especially to my "brother," Charlie Davis.

I and my friends also enjoyed the summer outdoor activities that NYC had to offer, such as the Outdoor New York Philharmonic "Concerts in the Parks" Series held in June. I especially look forward to Jazzmobile's Great Jazz on the Hill, which was held in mid-August in uptown Central Park.

There was also the Urban League Football Classic at Giants Stadium in East Rutherford, New Jersey.

We lost Charlie Davis in his sleep on Sunday morning following the 2018 CIAA tournament. May God bless him and his family!

For this event, in 2007, we and WWRL 1600 hosted a private suite reception benefiting The Urban League with activities that included a marching band competition at halftime and cookouts and partying in the Meadowlands parking lot. Among the invited guests were Ros; Charlie D. and some of the Boys High crew; Mike Hill and his sister Diane; Toni G.; and WWRL's Denise E. and her family. We were also greeted by my old neighbor from Queens, NY Urban League's Jeff Burns, who stopped by to check on us. What a great afternoon of fun, games, and refreshments.

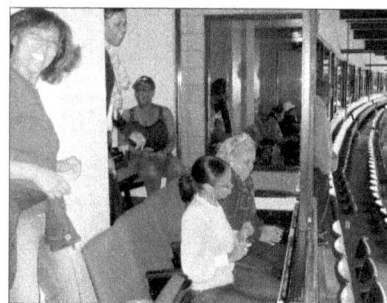 

Enjoying NY Urban League HBCU Football Classic

Giants Stadium tailgate party

GIVING PEOPLE A REASON TO BE CHEERFUL

During the freezing months in the northeast after the NFL Super Bowl season was over, the doldrums tended to overtake everyone. They were tired of boots and slushy weather and longed for spring.

In the winter of 2009 (when President Obama had just taken office), just after I had finished a ski commitment to our sponsors at the NBS (National Brotherhood of Skiers) out west, I wondered what to organize next. "How about a 'cabin fever' retreat weekend in Florida," I thought. "Now that sounds like a good idea." After checking out some weekend rates, I and my team (Virgie Baptiste and her crew) decided on the West Palm Beach area since a friend of ours, Barbara Cheives, had moved there some years before. Barbara is a very popular figure there.

Our Cabin Fever Retreat Weekend in downtown
West Palm Beach area of shops & restaurants

We had met her during the many years she had spent visiting her aunt, who lived next door to our mom in Queens. She supplied us with local tourist information and encouraged us to stay at the West Palm Beach Marriott, which was close to the shops, clubs, and restaurants of Cityplace. She even offered a shuttle to the beach.

Many of our folks in New York thought this was a fun interruption to the drab winter, and they booked not just the weekend, but a couple of days before to extend their stays. They even ventured outside our itinerary to the casino and on water excursions. We organized dinner plans at different restaurants and cocktails at The Blue Martini club. Singles, couples and small groups joined during this short but enjoyable winter getaway.

The Dow Twins always had lot of trips and events. In May of 2009 Harold Dow scheduled a fun-in-the-sun excursion to West Palm Beach, Florida with lots of activities. After settling in our hotel, we decided to take a taxi to Palm Beach, where the seashore was located. The drive took twenty minutes, and we were surprised to learn that taxis were not permitted to cross the Royal Park Bridge into Palm Beach proper because of zoning laws that seemed to be intended to deter tourists from this exclusive area. I and my friends were not deterred. We walked across the quarter mile bridge and another ten minutes to the beach on the other side.

We were excited about getting to this beach, especially because of its exclusivity—it seemed intended only for the wealthy residents of Palm Beach. Most excited was one of my girlfriends, who was a sun goddess. When we arrived, the water was beautiful, but there were no trees for shade and no chair or umbrella rentals—we assumed, again, to deter tourists. So, we set our towels down on the sand in the hot sun and relaxed for a couple of hours. By then we were hungry, and tired from being in the sun.

The ten-minute walk going back to the bridge felt like miles. In addition to being overheated and hungry, we were also thirsty.

As we approached the bridge, we felt really drained. About two-thirds of the way across, we heard an alarm ringing and realized that this was a drawbridge, which we hadn't noticed before, being true New Yorkers. The alarm meant that we only had a few minutes to get the rest of the way across before the bridge lifted up to allow boats to pass. I started walking really fast, but when I looked behind me I realized one of my girlfriends was walking too slowly. My adrenaline started pumping since I knew we were running out of time, and I started shouting for my girlfriend to pick up the pace or get left behind. She barely made it before the bridge started to rise.

Deterrents aside, this was a beautiful trip and we had lots of fun.

Virgie Baptiste

Later in that trip another memorable incident occurred poolside at the hotel. I was walking by the pool and saw Virgie's "sun goddess" friend lounging in the heat. I noticed a burning smell and asked, "What tanning lotion did you put on?" She told me that a Harlem merchant had sold her shea butter to tan with, and I quickly explained that she smelled like she was cooking, and that shea butter offered no sun protection! She realized that she was, indeed, burning and not tanning and hurried back to her room to wash off. Never take a city merchant's word for anything beach related.

Diana, Denise and Virgie in West Palm Beach, Florida
for Sunday brunch and art show

Our get away "cabin fever" weekend in West Palm Beach always featured something new to attend. On one trip one of our guests, Hollie, and I happened upon an old friend: Seth Anderson. He was from NYC, but had moved to Florida years before and taken a job at the airport in Systems.

When we inquired about the nature of his work, he stated that he programed the flights for pilots on 737 passenger airlines; then he asked if we were interested in trying out a flight simulator used to train commercial pilots. Of course, we said yes, and he took us to a facility near the airport. After giving us a tour, he invited us into one of the simulators. My friend Hollie agreed to be my co-pilot seat, and I sat in the pilot's seat.

At one of our Florida "Cabin Fever" trips, Vicky, Hollie and flight engineer Seth Anderson invited us to do a simulator session in a A320 cabin. Unbelievable experience!

As the flight engineer, Seth programmed the plane to fly under my control from Newark airport to Kennedy airport over the Hudson River and the New York skyline. After setting the simulator program, he instructed us on how to maneuver the aircraft. We, the so-called pilot and co-pilot, were very excited and nervous with all the instructions he'd given us; plus, now we were sealed in the cockpit like real pilots. As we looked at screens, we had the actual impression that we were taking off in flight.

At this point, my co-pilot Hollie decided that the "fake" flight was much too real for her, and she abandoned her seat. Not willing to give in to the pressure of flying in this commercial airline simulator, I kept going. Seth could see how nervous I was because, unbeknownst to me, my shoulders had tensed up so much they were practically touching my ears (even though I thought I was acting calm). Seth told me to relax my shoulders. "You're doing fine," he reassured me.

What a tremendous experience, being in the cockpit. Maneuvering turns was especially exciting. You had to turn a small dial to make the plane bank left or right; and most importantly while banking, you simultaneously had to power up the engine so the nose of the airplane didn't dip down, potentially causing a crash.

"Flying" from Newark to JFK in the simulator, I could see the Long Island Expressway with the white and red lights of the traffic; then I flew around to the Rockaways to set up the landing pattern. The next day, upon actually flying back to New York, we were on the same type of plane we'd used in the simulator. It was a great experience that neither Holly nor I will ever forget any time soon. *Many thanks to Seth Anderson for that unforgettable flight!*

Looking back, the many excursions that we organized and participated in over a lifetime brought so much joy to

Norman Dow escorting Stevie Wonder into TBOF's Bogard's nightclub

our lives and to those of our friends and supporters. A sampling of our travel agenda over time includes England, France and Amsterdam in 1976; Acapulco, Mexico for summer getaways throughout the 1980s; skiing in Europe with Vinny's Long Island Educators group between 1981 and 1990; skiing the northwestern and eastern coasts of the US and Canada with the NBS (National Brotherhood of Skiers) in February and March between 1989 and 2007; the trip of a lifetime to Japan's Nagano Olympic Ski Resort and China's Great Wall and Olympic Stadium in Beijing in 2008; cabin fever retreat weekends to West Palm Beach, Florida from 2009 to 2014; and the CIAA Basketball Tournaments with the Boys High crew in Charlotte, North Carolina between 2015 and 2018. *All reasons to be cheerful!*

Ran into Essence's Susan Taylor hosting her book, In the Spirit, at the NBS Summit gathering out west in the '90s

Bermuda Prime Minister, Jennifer Smith (seated center), enjoying a reunion of her New York City longtime friends

Club Promoter's FAM trip to examine the positive trips to the West Indian Islands: Jimi Holloway, Harold Dow, Herman M., Coordinator Carl Bartlett and Kevin Boyce

Lady DJ Wells playing at one of our most popular Uptown MASKquerade parties

One of the most popular "Reasons to be Cheerful" events: our MASKquerade Parties

The Farrington family, longtime supporters and neighbors in Queens, at one of our MASKquerade Parties

One of our biggest supporters and friends, Earline Jenkins, plus her MASKed crew

Harold Dow honored by Queens Borough President Melinda Katz's Business Award

CHAPTER FIVE

Building the Brand

Hit Songs

"Good Times" by CHIC

"Get Down on It" by Kool & The Gang

"Gonna Make You Sweat" ("Everybody Dance Now") by C+C Factory

---

Since the establishment of The Dow Twins as a national social entertainment brand in 1971, Norman and I made its cultivation a top priority.

We conceived of our professional identity while we were students at St. John's University, where everyone knew us as "The Twins, Harold and Norman," so we decided that our name should be our brand. We knew that, because our family name was our brand, we had to ensure that it was always associated with excellence; and that it was unique—distinct from any competitors.

We came up with our first logo; added a sketch of our yellow Volkswagen; and started handing out 8"x10" flyers to announce our presence in the social event market. Every school holiday or pre-holiday, we would host a party primarily for the students that could neither afford to go home or on vacation. It turned out to be a great idea and, *wow*, what turnouts we had!

Our reputation and business quickly grew due to our university student networking strategies and the success of our many well-attended social events. As I mentioned in Chapter 2, upon graduation in 1973, when the Disco Era was just getting started, we noticed that our older bowling buddies—The Best of Friends—were taking the New York City party scene by storm. They were bringing people together by hosting events in small clubs in Queens and in hotel ballrooms and other venues in Manhattan.

Norman and I decided to see how our pals were doing, so we went to one of their venues—La Martinique on 57th Street and Sixth Avenue in Midtown—for an afterwork party on a weekday and, as they say, "the joint was jumping." Norman and I were very impressed by what we saw, and we strategized how we might duplicate their success with our younger market.

In those early years, we knew that an important branding strategy in our business was the quality of the music. We tested several DJs that we had learned about from the numerous events we'd attended, and we settled on Pete DJ Jones, who performed with his wife, Becky. Norman dubbed Pete "the first real rapper" because of his ability to sing along with the songs and add his "two cents" over the beats to keep people entertained. Remember, this was years before the first rap songs were released. Pete would also ID each song and alert the audience to the different genres of music that were coming up next. People loved Pete's style, and he knew how to get them up on the dance floor.

Our amazing lead DJs were essential to building The Dow Twins brand. From our beginnings with Pete DJ Jones and Becky; then with Carl TNT with his amazing sound system; followed by

Derrick Gaines and Reggie Wells, who kept Othello and Justine's jumping; later, New York City's "It's Got to Be" Tommie Allen, until his untimely passing in 2020; and finally, Lady DJ Wells. Norman and I were always determined to hire only the best.

Note from a Fan:

Hi, Harold,

It's Carol Woods' sister, Cherie, from what I call your PA (Pennsylvania) family. I just want you to know what a fabulous time I had on Thursday (at the Copacabana). Even though we were late, we were still able to take advantage of that delicious meal after a long and stressful trip from PA. I'd never been to a Black affair where there was enough food to feed everyone. Then, to experience Lady DJ Wells for the first time. <u>Speechless! Breath-taking!</u>

You guys may be used to this, but it was an absolute treat for me. Thank you for a great time. Looking forward to next year.

Cherie Simpson

In order to continue building our brand, Norman and I saved money from every venture so that we could begin investing in larger and more elegant venues to host our friends. Meanwhile, TBOF were building out their own nightclub—Leviticus—in a leased space in the shadow of the Empire State Building on 33rd Street (the name "Leviticus" came from the Third Book of Moses in the Bible about the slave Exodus from Egypt and God's teachings given to Moses).

As you've read, when they took an option on a second leased space on Eighth Ave and 35th Street, TBOF member Tony Cooper (a fellow bowler in Queens) asked if my brother and I would be interested in managing their second club. At the same time, we received a similar request from the Reese Company, which owned Steak and Brew establishments on 34th and 42nd streets. We had to make a decision and we chose, as you know, to go with The Best of Friends because we felt we knew them better.

The name Othello (the Black nobleman and military general from Shakespeare's play) was suggested, and the location was developed as the new home of The Dow Twins. Now our brand was associated with major Black party-developers in New York City.

Fashionable young ladies enjoying a beverage from our sponsor

As club managers and evolving entrepreneurs, we aimed for a new level of success not only for TBOF, who had entrusted us with their new venue, but for ourselves as well. Before, during and after our tenure at Othello (later Justine's), a key branding goal was to create "Hot Events." What's a Hot Event, you might ask? It's one where the music is tight, the date is ideal for high volume attendance, the theme is fitting and fun, and the venue is elegant.

In the early 1970s, we chose a funky club like The Late Show in Greenwich Village, or an afterwork bar like The Iron Horse in Penn Station; not to mention Leviticus and Justine's. In the 1980s, it was the South Street Seaport, the aircraft carrier USS Intrepid, the Copacabana, the Chelsea mega club 1018, or Club Broadway on the Upper West Side. Each event was marketed with a chic invitation flier to draw the right kind of crowd. We hired the best graphic designers at our disposal to make this happen; our "Hot Events" were as diverse as our imaginations.

A reality that spurred us to come up with new and better concepts was the fact that the nightclub business is very fickle. What works in one place doesn't always work in another. This was one of the reasons why the name Othello was changed to Justine's in the late seventies—so that the club could feel and became more successful. Why was this so? Many thought it had to do with the renovations and new "lounge" vibe we created for Justine's with a pool table, backgammon tables and comfortable seating. Others thought it was our new assistant manager, Justice, who was then (and always) at the top of her game. Still others believed it was timing—Justine's became a sister club to the new Leviticus, and the two venues shared clientele. Whatever it was, it worked for a time in the competitive and congested eighties Midtown Manhattan nightclub scene.

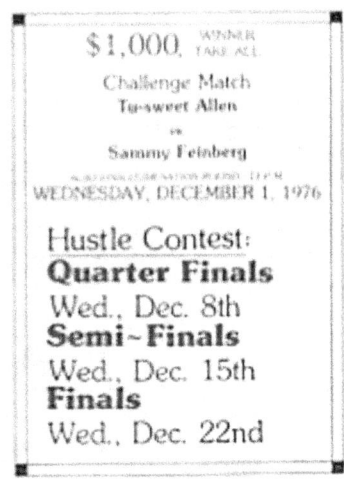

Our 1976 Hustle Contest at Othello's NYC

Salsa Fridays After Work at Justine's

To keep Justine's fresh, we added live Latin music to the experience of dancing, with parties that quickly evolved into popular staple events that lasted for years. It brought together the Black and Latinx crowds, and others from Queens to New Jersey and from Uptown to the Eastside. Our people bonded around these Latin music affairs.

The popularity of "Salsa Friday's" was such that it turned into a regular weekly friends' gathering spot for many. It also hosted birthday and anniversary celebrations with live Latin bands that cherished the opportunity to be featured at a Midtown club in NYC. And, of course, the music had to be the best. Some of Norman's favorite groups, Bobby Rodriquez y La Campania, Manny Oquendo's Conjunto Libre, and Tito Puente and his band were featured in the first series of dances.

The Latin bands would arrive early to set up their instruments and do sound checks, so that they'd be ready when the doors opened. They were also interviewed on Spanish-speaking radio stations regarding their appearance at the popular Justine's nightclub. Many people in the New York City community recognized "Salsa Friday's" as one of the first events to bring the African American and Latinx  adult market together for dancing and socializing. More importantly, the heightened PR we received as a result of this bit of innovative branding was ever-so-helpful to the sustainability of the club in the unpredictable era of disco in the city.

The South Street Seaport

The South Street Seaport was another favorite and ground-breaking venue choice. The revitalized Seaport neighborhood and piers were completed between 1983 and 1985 with European-style markets, restaurants and shopping. It was located on the East Side of southern Manhattan, opposite the World Trade Center's Twin Towers, which were on the West Side.

As the new hot spot in New York City, we decided to take advantage of the Seaport to penetrate the Wall Street / World Trade Center (WTC) crowd. Roebling's restaurant and bar on the mezzanine level of the Fulton Fish market was our introduction. We convinced the owner to rent us his space, and he quickly realized what a unique African American clientele we had. We decided to host a major afterwork series on Fridays, using the entire space of the rooftop Museum Club (an open space with seating, a dance area, and a wraparound terrace for summer viewing of the seaport village).

After a slow spring season start, the Wall Street, WTC, Midtown, and Queens crowd finally arrived in late June. The results were a huge success for us (with the help of our prime promoters, Harold DH, Al Florant, and L. Greg Smith Groups). All of this came about because the owner of Roebling's restaurant took a chance on a young African American organization. Not only did we increase his revenue, but we exposed many people to a new eatery in the South Street Seaport area.

Carl TNT spinning the tunes at Roeblings in the Seaport

Bob Belle at Roeblings speaking to the guys & future Congressman Meeks enjoying the sights

New Years Eve at The Museum Club, South Street Seaport, NYC

A Day at the Races

"A Day at the Races" at Belmont Racetrack was yet another of our Hot Event branding concepts. For many years, my Mom gave an annual Mother's Day event at Belmont Racetrack under the name "Les Amies," with the help of her friends Frances White and Vivian Carney. Early in 2001, Norman and I took over organizing the event and moved it to Father's Day, which many of the ladies loved. It allowed them to treat their fathers to a fun day, instead of just giving him another tie or bottle of cologne. My Mom and her friends could now come to the event as guests and enjoy the holiday without having to do the work of coordinating everything.

Our pitch was, "Are you tired of looking for a fun activity for Father's Day where you are not rushed out of the restaurant? Then spend the afternoon with us." We averaged 100 folks every year and were always given the same section in the beautiful Garden Terrace restaurant on the main Clubhouse floor, with reserved seating. The early breakfast buffet, the later brunch, and the convenience of just walking a few steps between the food and the betting windows was a win-win.

Annual Day at the Races, Belmont Racetrack

The staff at the racetrack treated us extra special when they realized that the Dow family had supported Belmont for so many years. They even sent cards and well wishes when I had my critical aorta attack in 2018.

By 2022, the demand for a Day at the Races was massive after two years of the COVID-19 lockdown without the Belmont excursion. We hosted our largest crowd ever, with the help of Dorita Clarke and friends, of over 150 folks. Many races were won.

Thanks to Harold and Norman for all the little things, and all the big things, too.

Being a widow since 2002, it was difficult to go out by myself, but that changed when I went to The Dow Twins Strata/Metronome nightclub and Intrepid events. I could always count on knowing at least one person there; and I could always count on getting a warm reception at the door. It didn't matter if I used my cane or my motorized wheelchair: by just showing up I knew I was going to have a fabulous time.

The girlfriends that joined me couldn't wait to come to each of The Twins' next events. Some were torn between doing what their husbands wanted to do for Father's Day or coming to one of The Twins' events, like Belmont's Day at the Races, where they would have a wonderful time. But they had to give their husbands at least the one day (smile). Thanks for the invitations to all your wonderful events and for the bonuses that you extended to me.

Mercedes Youman, June 4th, 2009

The MASKquerade Balls

Norman and I were also known for our unique MASKquerade Balls at various locations. One of the first was held as a costume and mask event in the spring of 1989 and was announced as "an evening of mystery and adventure." Always on the lookout for new and exciting venues, we found the Octagon nightclub on West 33rd Street.

The event went well, even though management tried to use metal detector wands on our guests, which I told them wasn't necessary. We assured them that we would cancel the event on the spot if they didn't suspend their wanding policy at once. They suspended the policy. We were strict about club owners' staff trying to search our folks for no reason. We didn't advertise on the radio or promote to an unvetted "Bridge and Tunnel" crowd. We informed all club owners that ours was a private membership, Black-owned special events company; that we knew our folks well; and that we never had a problem.

First annual MASKquerade Party

In 2001, we decided to upend our MASKquerade Balls. We changed the date and time to afterwork during the late October Halloween season (strategically scheduled about eight weeks after the annual USS Intrepid end-of-summer gala, when our followers were ready for another fête). We changed the location to the West 34th Street Copacabana site, and we altered the concept from costumes to colorful masks only, alongside all-black attire so that the mystique was in the mask you wore. This allowed men and women to go to work dressed in black attire and just add a mask to their outfit at the door.

Many smiles at our annual MASKed affair

The ladies came with all types of colorful masks, or we would supply fancy feathered masks purchased from New Orleans Bayou area at a small cost. Some of the more creative ladies who traveled to different countries abroad brought unique handmade masks back with them just for the event. Women especially loved it and enjoyed walking around mysteriously wearing their new masks. Some even donned their disguises ahead of time and walked from the train station at 34th Street up to Eleventh Avenue with their masks on, in a scenic parade that created a buzz on the street. The gentlemen were a little more reserved, but would pull out their masks at the door, adding to the air of mystery.

At around 8:30 p.m., we would host a "Best Male and Female Masks" contest, after which everyone discarded their masks for the remainder of the evening. It was always a fun event, and it became an annual one in the years that followed.

BUILDING THE BRAND

Gemini & Cancer Birthday Celebrations

Not surprisingly, my brother and I loved celebrating our birthday, and we decided to turn our birthday season into another Hot Event: our "Gemini & Cancer Birthday Celebrations." It all started with our birthday celebration at Othello in the 1970s. We realized then how many Geminis and Cancers we knew. The Geminis loved to have fun with their friends, and the Cancers, though sometimes less outgoing than Geminis, were more than willing to participate in the festivities.

At locations from Club Broadway on West 96th Street to Strata / Metronome on East 21st Street, our friends enjoyed socializing and being the center of attention every summer in May, June, or July. Most of the birthday folks had been our friends for many years, and I will always be grateful for the friendships that Norman and I enjoyed from all of them.

Tian at the Riverbank Grill Restaurant

Tian at the Riverbank Grill was a Latin-Asian fusion restaurant and bar in Riverbank State Park in Harlem that I discovered in 2011 (it was formerly NY Knicks Earl Monroe's "Pearl's" restaurant). It was my first venture into an inventive Hot Event that combined an early evening casual dinner with an after-dinner dance experience that culminated at one o'clock in the morning. Never afraid to try something new for our loyal patrons, the Tian venue allowed us to go Uptown for the first time. The response

165

was overwhelming, especially for our Bronx and Westchester crowd who lived north of Manhattan and who were happy, for a change, not to have to venture all the way into Midtown.

Another attractive aspect of the new site was the fact that people could enjoy an opportunity to start their evening early and get back home at a reasonable hour, so that they were fresh for church or other Sunday morning activities (tennis anyone?). Also, our patrons were forty years older than they had been when we started, and staying up all night was not as much fun as it used to be (smile).

The former NY Knick and co-owner of 'The Pearl' Earl Monroe and Harold Dow

It was no simple feat to ensure that our dinner guests placed their orders before 8:00 p.m. so that they'd have their food served no later than by 9:00 p.m.; but timing was everything since the dance party had to start

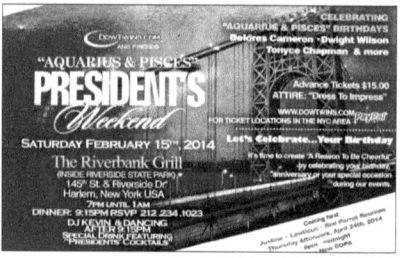

by 10:00 p.m. Also, we had to make sure that the non-diners had access to any available seating. Since this wasn't a disco (it was a restaurant), it could only handle about 200 people max, it had limited dining space, and a small bar area. Plus, Tian at the Riverbank Grill was not a preferred destination: it was well off Riverside Parkway, and you had to turn into the park entrance at 145th Street to access the venue.

But these challenges made it all the more fun to orchestrate. I and my team managed to accommodate everyone, and between advertising, word of mouth and street buzz, our loyal followers—from Uptown to Downtown and from Brooklyn to Queens—ventured out to see this new venue of ours. The enterprise worked.

Family gatherings hosted at Tian
at the Riverbank Grill in Upper Manhattan, NYC

We hosted a monthly event at Tian at the Riverbank Grill that, weather permitting, included an outdoor patio setting for cocktails and finger food with a spectacular view of the Hudson River and the George Washington Bridge, which was lit up nightly. To our surprise and delight, folks started having birthday celebrations at Tian instead of in their homes, which increased finger food sales even after 9:00 p.m.

In the warmer months we called it "The Sunset by the River Series." Our Uptown foray lasted five years, after which new management renamed the restaurant Sofrito with an exclusively Latin menu. It was great fun while it lasted.

Our first National Promotion outside the NY area for the Spinks campaign in New Orleans

BUILDING THE BRAND

The Dow Twins' A-Team: John Taylor, Tommie Allen, Justice Vasquez and Harold A. Dow

In building our brand, Norman and I wanted to orchestrate spectacular up-market events that African Americans had rarely, if ever, had the opportunity to enjoy because of the discrimination, exclusionism and stereotypes that had barred Black folks from so many "White" venues in the past. Our brand became associated with opening up as many doors as possible for our folks to have fun.

Harold, especially, loved and appreciated creating special and successful events in new and interesting venues. But what both Twins were masters of was creating and growing their own unique brand. They were GOATs at promotion, with a track record to prove it. Anybody can open a restaurant, club or bar. But to keep it hot, successful and flourishing with such a loyal following for so many years is a phenomenal accomplishment not matched by many.

THE DOW TWINS' LEGACY

I learned a lot from each of these three: Norman (RIP), Harold (still my bestie), and Justice (not just my friend, but my sister). Those were golden years. And they changed my life.

Dawne Steward Walton

BUILDING THE BRAND

TAKE THE DOW TWINS PARTY SURVEY!

(Just for fun! Circle your answer)

1. Which do you consider The Dow Twins' Hottest Club of the '80s?
- Strata on Fifth Avenue
- The Copa on 57th Street
- La Maganette on Third Avenue

Another venue: _____

2. Who do you consider The Dow Twins' Hottest DJ of the '90s?
- Reggie Wells
- Bert Morgan
- Tommie Allen

Another DJ: _____

3. What do you considered the Hottest Song played at The Dow Twins' parties in the '80s?
- Love is the Message
- Let's Celebrate
- Thriller

Another song: _____

4. Given the choice, which mode of dance would you enjoy the most?
- The New York Hustle
- The Bus Stop
- The Latin Salsa

Another style of dance: _____

5. If you could only attend one event, which would you attend?
- The Seaport's Museum Club
- USS Intrepid Museum
- The 34th Street Copacabana

Another Dow Twins event: _____

CHAPTER SIX

The Sports We Loved

Hit Songs

"Say It Loud—I'm Black and I'm Proud" by James Brown

"Show Me Love" by Robin S.

"Love is the Message" by MFSB

Up to now, it might seem that Norman and I worked 24/7. Granted, sometimes we did, but it wasn't all work and no play. We enjoyed our leisure time, which generally involved sports of one type or another. Our favorites were bowling, skiing, tennis and, as spectators, Formula One Racing—non-traditional pastimes for Black men; but then, there wasn't much about me or my brother that was traditional.

We first got the sports bug during our childhood days in Jamaica when Norman and I had a routine: we went from the Cub Scouts to the park for baseball and then bowling. Although bowling, tennis and skiing were our favorite sports, we also did a bit of swimming, but not with the same dedication. Norman and I swam in elementary school on St. Catherine's swim team, and we loved the ocean. We would travel to Jones beach with our friends on the weekends, where Norman and I became good body surfers, using the waves as they would break to carry us to shore (great fun).

Once we grew up, most of our travels to warm destinations included beach time, especially in Acapulco, Mexico and West Palm Beach or Miami in Florida. That said, our first real love was bowling.

Bowling

Bowling was the activity that followed us through high school and college. Our parents introduced us to the sport, and we bowled every chance we got. As "mirror" twins, one of us was left-handed and the other right-handed. In bowling, Norman naturally threw a deep hook from the left side, and I a soft curve from the right. Other than the names on our team shirts, most folks we bowled with paid attention to which hand we used in order to tell us apart.

As I remember, in high school and much of college we were the only Black bowlers in the school leagues. In fact, we were Varsity Lettermen in bowling at Christ the King High School and at St. John's University, where I was team captain for three years.

After meeting The Best of Friends, we were happy to learn that they loved to bowl as much as we did, and we were able to keep the trend going for a few more years. Norman was a strong striker and usually won high game. He could string five or six strikes in a row, and sometimes more. My specialty was spares and maybe a double strike on occasion. I could nine-spare you to death, so my average stayed around 196 in my junior and senior years at St. John's.

At that time (1971-1973) 196 was a high scoring average in the college ranks at Bowlmor Lanes in downtown Manhattan; but my score wasn't enough to allow me to go pro after college because I didn't bowl enough strikes in a row. I didn't mind, though, since Norman and I were both looking forward to expanding our new event planning business into the city. Pro bowling wasn't really on the agenda. Array

Our bowling teams from high school to college

Tennis

Norman and I learned to play tennis in the early 1970s at the Liberty Park courts in Queens. These were public courts and in terrible shape, so we decided to participate in a protest that blocked traffic on Liberty Avenue to draw attention to the fact that the tennis courts there were in need of major repairs and resurfacing. Our complaints sparked the interest of local politicians, and the courts and lights were overhauled. Even then, we weren't satisfied with anything but the best. Also, it was the early '70s, when protesting was a way of life for Black folks.

Although not as hazardous as skiing, tennis had its dangers, too. Once while playing with our best friend from grammar school, Vinny Scott, I rolled my ankle so badly that my nurse friend Betty Clark had to take me to Queens hospital. My ankle was the size of a small cantaloupe. Once at the hospital, Betty went searching for a doctor while hospital staff put me in a wooden wheelchair with my leg raised.

Before Betty could get back, I passed out inexplicably and flipped the wheelchair on its side. At this point, my pulse was so weak that the nurses literally ripped my tennis shirt off and rushed me into the ER. They laid me on a gurney and the doctor was about to hit me with the defibrillator paddles when Betty saw that my eyes were rolling around in a panic and stopped him. In my mind I was shouting, "Don't shock me! I'm awake!"

In fact, I was semiconscious and having a vision of myself looking down at my prone body from above. The hospital staff told me later that they thought I'd had an "out of body experience" for a moment. Meanwhile, the doctor was wondering why my pulse was so weak, since this wasn't a normal reaction from a badly-sprained ankle. "Has he eaten? Is he dehydrated?"

I was lucid enough to tell the doctor that I had been fasting to lose weight. To which the doctor responded, "Well, that was a dumb idea! And that's why your ankle injury sent your body into cardiac arrest. You're very lucky!" I could hardly believe what he was saying. Cardiac arrest! That was one close call. Who says tennis isn't dangerous?

THE SPORTS WE LOVED

The US Open Greeters were always happy to see us each year. Smile!

THE DOW TWINS' LEGACY

Our hero, NY Mayor David N. Dinkins, who personally saved the US Open by hosting it at Flushing Meadows Grounds and diverted airplane flyovers from LaGuardia Airport. Like us, a longtime tennis lover

Tennis star Madison "Maddy" Keys with Harold Dow at The U.S. Open Tennis Complex

This very close call aside, over the years tennis has been my recovery tool to get back in shape after any hiatus—illness, surgery or otherwise. Tennis has always been an important physical and mental therapy for me. I especially look forward to enjoying tennis since, unlike skiing, which is a seasonal sport only viable for about two months a year in the Northeast, tennis can be played year-round. I play doubles mostly, particularly since I've had two knee surgeries, but that's fine with me; it's still a good workout.

Over the last few years, though, everything has been about pickleball. The soon-to-be retired tennis pros, young people, and the less-able senior citizens (for whom pickleball was meant, but who can hardly get court time) are all gravitating towards it. Even the Detective Kevin Williams (DKW) Liberty Tennis courts in Queens are being redesigned for partial pickleball courts in the future.

Despite this, now in 2023, I'm still telling my doctors, "Do whatever you have to do, just so long as I can keep playing tennis!"

Skiing

As early as 1978, Norman and I hosted our first ski weekend trip to Jiminy Peak in the West Mountains of New York State. A group of us went by bus for a reasonable price (an incentive for our guests) and, even though more people partied than skied, it opened a new outlet for us and other adventurous folks in our circle.

By the early 1980s, we decided to travel east to ski Europe with our friend, Vinny Scott (his father, Oscar, had been a top bowler in his day as a member of the Gothamite's Invitational Bowling Club where we were also members).

Vincent, who had become a science teacher, was taking a group of students to Europe and invited us to join him afterwards so he could introduce us to European skiing. He encouraged us to go skiing all over Europe, which we did from 1981 to 1990.

> Once we all were somewhat established professionally, we started skiing. Norman, Harold and I loved it.
>
> A memorable early experience occurred with Harold. I was teaching at the time, and was asked to chaperone some students on a trip to Germany. Harold mentioned that he would like to take a trip to Europe, too. He suggested that I meet him after I finished chaperoning. We posed the idea to Norman, who had no desire to travel anywhere at the time, so Harold decided to go without him (just a note—they were always together. At home at their mother's house, they shared a room. Even later in life, they sometimes shared a room. So, this was a departure).
>
> Harold met me in Paris, and although we argued non-stop over money (Harold wanted to pool our money, but I had

spent almost everything I had before he got there), for the most part, we had a memorable time. My fondest memories are of Amsterdam's red-light district, Anne Frank's house, and all the museums. This trip sealed my bond with Harold. I look back on it even now and smile.

Over the years, we traveled all around the world, skiing in places like Austria, Italy and Switzerland. The Barker twins (Andrea and Annette from our childhood) joined us and introduced Norman and Harold to the National Brotherhood of Skiers (NBS). The Twins ended up promoting for NBS and bringing new sponsors to them.

Vincent Scott

Before taking on Europe, Norman and I were initiated at a ski school in the picture-postcard destination of Mont Tremblant in Canada. We had a five-day intensive training course there, which prepared us for some unconventional European skiing on unmarked trails that sometimes led across a national border from one country to another.

On our first European ski tour, we joined more than forty educators from Vinny's school in Long Island. They were a fun bunch to ski with. They were fearless, and experienced skiers, but very helpful to us when we needed them. For instance, they helped us to navigate the habit that Europeans had of crowding you when you were getting in line for the lift. This meant they were scratching their skis on top of yours, which American skiers did not tolerate. Scratching someone else's skis on purpose was almost cause for fighting as far as American skiers were concerned. "Don't scratch my skis!"

Norman Dow skiing in Europe between 1981 – 1989

We were fortunate to learn how to ski; and we encouraged other friends to follow suit and enjoy the world through the lens of this great sport. We had been skiing in Europe for ten years with our best friends, Vincent and Thomas Copeland, before we decided to add ski vacations to our brand. The idea came to us after our little sisters, the Barker twins (Andrea and Annette) persuaded us to attend the 1989 National Brotherhood of Skiers (NBS) Summit at Steamboat Springs, Colorado. Norman and I were pleasantly surprised by the incredible number of Black folks attending the Summit. We met people from all over the country: Miami, New Orleans, Kansas City, and even from states that had very few people of color.

That year, greatly influenced by the Barker sisters, Norman and I ventured west to ski "Black." Yes, there were Black skiers and Black ski clubs all around the country, enjoying the sport and traveling together. We joined the NBS, which was organized into four regional areas; it was one of the largest ski organizations in America.

The NBS summer retreat to Miami, Florida

From 1991 to 2006, we partnered with the NBS for their Summits to help enhance their internationally-renowned ski conventions with top quality, engaging and unique networking opportunities for guests convening in Vail and Steamboat, Colorado, as well as in Park City, Utah and many other acclaimed resort sites in eastern and western Canada.

One of the quirks associated with skiing "Black" was the amount of clothing required. We quickly learned that this had nothing to do with staying warm, but rather with staying fashionable, both on and off the slopes. Previously, when we had traveled with Vinny in Europe, one ski outfit plus dungarees and sweatshirts had been adequate. When we traveled with the Black skiers, multiple ski outfits and evening attire for the many social events were required, which meant a lot of additional luggage.

Evening themed events were very popular and required Western, African, and lingerie outfits for the week-long ski trips (luckily, we were well-informed of NBS's popular themed events in advance of our first trip with them to Steamboat Springs, Colorado.)

As fate would have it, the following year in 1990 at the NBS Summit in Salt Lake City, Utah we ran into a friend from New York: Andre Harrell. He was founder of Uptown Records (and discovered Sean "P. Diddy" Combs and Mary J. Blige). He had arrived the week before to promote his first film project, *Strictly Business* featuring Halle Berry, at the Sundance Film Festival. He heard that over 4,000 Black skiers were arriving at the end of the week and decided to stay on.

Andre had the idea that Norman and I should host a gathering at his massive Utah mansion. The plan was to invite one hundred of our ski friends, and his crew would do the same with their circle.

Unfortunately, a couple of days before the party Andre was injured in a snowmobile accident and had to leave, but his partner from his rap duo Dr. Jeckyll & Mr. Hyde, Alonzo Brown, stayed on to host the event on Friday.

In skier's tradition, the folks bought plenty of food and beverages for a fun evening of mixing and mingling. Even the State Police helped navigate the NBS guests to our location. This impromptu event in Utah elevated The Dow Twins brand to a national level. Folks from all over the country were talking about the fabulous party they attended, given by some twins from New York at Andre and Alfonso's mansion in Utah. This event ensured us further Dow Twins / NBS events, sponsorships, and notoriety for many years to come, not to mention excellent skiing (sadly, Andre Harrell passed away in 2020 at age fifty-nine).

On one of my many skiing trips, the instructor was showing the group how to handle several tight moguls, including how to side-slide them. Well, my skis got away from me, and I started to slide backwards, falling on my own outstretched arm. I thought I heard a "pop" sound, but didn't feel any pain, so kept on skiing.

Upon ending the day, I noticed that my shoulder was a little sore, so I asked for a bag of ice before entering our motorcoach for the four-hour trip back home. It wasn't until months later that the true nature of the injury presented itself. My shoulder started hurting, and I rightly guessed that it had to do with my fall.

Our dear friend Doreen Johnson, who once promised my mom, "Don't worry about Harold, I got him!" had me. Doreen suggested that I see her favorite doctor, Answorth Allen, at the Hospital for Special Surgery. I later found out that Dr. Allen had performed surgery on the shoulder of one of my Long Island Railroad train mates (a tennis player) and on the foot of a neighbor from my apartment building.

THE DOW TWINS' LEGACY

Andre Harrell's crew, who hosted our first party
in Utah at their fabulous mansion

At one of our parties at the Delta Center in 1999,
the GM complimented us, saying that her son had never skied
or seen this many Black folks in his young life in Utah

The Barker twins, The Dow Twins and Tina / Randy girls enjoying a ski house in Vail, Colorado

Dr. Allen sent me for an MRI, which showed a fully-ruptured rotator cuff. Because I had iced the injury when it first occurred, I had stemmed any inflammation that might have caused major pain and immobility. Thus began a string of surgeries and mishaps that lasted the next eleven years and ended my ski life, but saved my tennis life. Thanks, Doreen!

As NBS members, in the early 1990s we introduced them to our own popular themed event—the MASKquerade Ball, which was well received. It featured masks shipped in from Mississippi and New Orleans Mardi Gras outlets. As announced in their newsletter, we also hosted the group's Mansion Party at Deer Valley in Utah, The Eagle Nest Party atop the Gondola at Vail in Colorado, and the Pre-Olympic Party at the Delta Center in Utah, to name only a few ski-related projects.

THE DOW TWINS' LEGACY

From: The National Brotherhood of Skiers Newsletter, 2004

"The Dow Twins' Annual Cooley High Reunion"

The New York City Flavor has been a force at the NBS since the early '90s, when The Dow Twins hosted their Mansion Party at Deer Valley Utah, The Eagle Nest Party atop the Gondola at Vail, and the Pre-Olympic Party at the Delta Center in Utah, to name a few.

This year, the evening is 'dedicated to those with discriminating taste,' featuring apple martinis and more. The DJ will include music from "Cooley High" oldies to salsa to reggae and yesterday's hits to today's hits. So, dress to impress and wear comfortable shoes to dance the night away … till 2:00 a.m. There will be prizes for best "Cooley High" outfits … male & female. **The Dow Twins & Friends** will do the rest.

We also were able to help with the NBS's entertainment by bringing a NYC-style of partying out West. This was done by incorporating more than one or two types of music in each event. To engage the Black ski crowd, our DJs played a mixture of oldies, contemporary, Latin and Caribbean sounds (with a couple of slow tunes thrown in for the lovers in the room). Whether it was contemporary, oldies, reggae, salsa, or ballads, there was something for everyone. No one wants to do line dancing or oldies all night long; variety is the best formula for a national audience out West.

Harold Dow, ready to ski   Norman Dow with Weldon Robinson and his ski buddy

With this formula, The Dow Twins parties were always well-received and attended. We also picked unique venues with spectacular views whenever possible.

Over the years, Norman and I had a blast, skiing the northeast with our buddies Tony Jerkins and Frasier, whom we roomed with for a weekend during the NBS Eastern Regional. One such weekend trip to Sunday River in Maine was sponsored by Remy Martin and, of course, it was a great weekend of skiing and après (after) ski gatherings.

The guys were in rare form. Frasier cooked breakfast, and top chef Jerkins prepared a quick but delicious dinner. Norman and I had cleanup duty, which was a pleasure after such meals. Tony took a lot of pride in his food preparation, and he made enough for us to invite a couple of ski honeys to join us. The ladies were very impressed with our coordination of dinner and cleanup just in time to hit the evening festivities together. We had many fun weekends with NBS.

As far as skiing was concerned, Frasier was the fearless one; Tony Jerkins and Norman were somewhat conservative skiers; and I tried to find any opportunity to "get air"—hitting a bump and flying over it. Sometimes Tony would forget who he was skiing with and, when he saw his ski partner "getting air," he'd realize it was me and not Norman.

Unfortunately, Norman and I never rose to the heights of the NBS ladies we skied with (like the Barker twins), but we had a great time trying—until they tried to convince us to jump off a ledge in 1998. That's where we drew the line! We saw some guys try that in Europe, and it didn't end well for them.

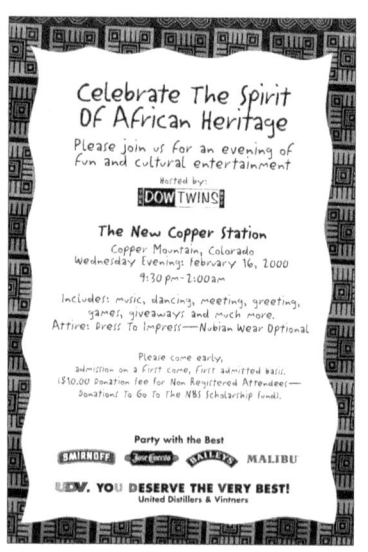

So, not only did skiing bring us years of personal fun, but professionally we were able to support the NBS by staging our brand of entertainment at their summits, New York style. Our unique events were supported not only by the NBS, but also by sponsorships from new players like *Alizé* in the beverage industry.

Our little sisters, Annette & Andrea, ready for a bike ride

Harold on a helicopter ride to DR airport

The Snoburners and friends are ready to enjoy a day of skiing

These parties were so well received that the NBS skiers looked forward to them annually; and we did not disappoint. We were truly blessed to have skied and participated in all those activities for over twelve years. The NBS celebrated their fiftieth anniversary in 2023 at Vail Mountain. Congrats!

After Norman's passing, it took about a year or so for me to feel comfortable enough to travel. Technically, I rarely skied or traveled without him, and even though friends offered to room with me, I wasn't interested. In 2007, though, the Sno Burners Ski club was planning a trip to Japan to ski the Olympic trails of Nagano. Before booking, the trip leader, Diane Moizio, suggested booking a second week in China.

I planned not to miss this opportunity to go, since I had missed the opportunity to travel with some my ski executives working in Cape Town and Sun City, South Africa, earlier. What a great decision. The fourteen-hour direct flight from JFK to Japan took place in 2008. The hotel was grand, the lodging very comfortable and most of the staff spoke English. The tour operator was first rate, informing us of all the sights, history, and new building going on in the city.

The highlight of the trip, of course, was skiing the great trails of Nagano. We had a wonderful time skiing and the weather cooperated, with mostly sunny days. The group was also acknowledged by Japanese's skiers, who clearly had never seen so many African Americans—and skiing, no less.

On the second leg of the trip to China, we had lucked out by arriving during the country's two week "no work" (national vacation) period, which meant that we had no heavy smog from excessive vehicles and factories to contend with.

In both countries, we had the opportunity to get wonderful massages, either going out to a spa, or getting them our room, or both. My choice was to do them both, but after fifty minutes of massaging from your scalp to your toes, I wasn't going anywhere but asleep.

When not relaxing after a massage, I had a chance to visit The Great Wall, Tiananmen Square, and to do some incredible shopping in China. Merchants had a unique policy of offering a small meal before entering their pearl and jade venues, which had you shopping and browsing comfortability. Diane Moizio served not only as the trip leader; she was also my savior when the shopping got a little heated between two vendors trying to sell me the same item—Diane would step in and resolve it.

THE SPORTS WE LOVED

We were on the second leg of a fabulous trip with friends and club members. We had already spent a week in Nagano, Japan, in the mountain site of the 1998 winter Olympic village.

Our tour guide, Tom, had dropped us off at what he called the "knock-off store," which was a multi-storied building with everything you could think of for sale, if you wanted to travel the shopping route. I had on a Spyder Club ski jacket. A young lady selling knock-off merchandise wanted me to look at her "Spyder" jackets. I was curious to see the difference, which was huge. She looked over and felt my jacket and said immediately, "Oh, yours is real. Never mind." She gave up trying to sell her knock-off to me at that point. But if you wanted to buy one or two for looks (not for warmth) they were cheap enough and came in fun colors.

One of the most memorable moments of the whole trip was when Harold came looking for me in my room at our hotel exclaiming, "I need you to come downstairs and be my wife!" He didn't mean it literally (smile). He needed me to pretend to be his wife so I could help him negotiate a price for another suitcase to replace one that had been damaged in transit. The proprietor told him to bring his wife so we could negotiate (woman to woman) a price for the luggage.

Well folks, I get downstairs, and the young lady asks, "Are you the wife?" and I say yes. She had a calculator in hand, and I had mine in hand also, so I could convert the currency. She gave me a price and I countered with, "Half," to which she said no.

We proceeded to haggle back and forth for a while. It was very intense. Both Harold and I started sweating and took off our hot ski jackets. I was beginning to think, "this isn't going to work," but it really was a nice bag, so I couldn't give up.

Finally, she gave us a price that was below what we wanted to settle for. "We'll take it," I said. I don't think I have ever haggled that hard over anything in my life (and I've done my fair share through the years). Then, as we were leaving another merchant said to us, "Come look at my bags, blah, blah …" giving us her typical pitch. She was a heavy-set woman and proceeded to jump up and down on a suitcase to show us how strong it was. Laughing hard Harold said to me, "Let's get the Hell out of here!"

Diane Moizio

Spectator Sports: Formula One Racing

Norman and I not only participated in sports, but we also had our favorite sports to watch as spectators—namely Formula One Racing, football and baseball. Even before Norman and I moved to Secaucus, NJ in 1983, we were very familiar with the Meadowlands area because of the Formula One races that took place there.

Annually, we would attend and watch the go-cart style race cars with their high-powered engines zoom around the track. We would invite friends to experience this internationally popular racing format. The ladies that we invited were so impressed with the power and sound of the race cars, driven by the likes of Mario Andretti, Emerson Fittipaldi, and Niki Lauda. These were exciting events.

Today, the most successful Formula One driver is Sir Lewis Hamilton from England, who drives for Mercedes. He won seven World Drivers' Championship titles, holds the records for the most wins, and he's Black, which makes watching Formula One that much more exciting.

As car enthusiasts, we chose to buy two Mercedes Benz 450 SLs in the mid-seventies, when few people knew anything about this Mercedes model. That was one of the best buys we ever made—and we found them in the *New York Times* used car section. Most people selling expensive cars through the *New York Times* back then were wealthy, took very good care of their vehicles, and didn't keep them for much more than three or four years.

Unbeknownst to us (and thanks to our cars), the word on the street was all about these rich Black twins who had opened a nightclub in Midtown and were parking their two-seater Mercedes Benzes out in front. Of course, that wasn't entirely true; we parked for most of the day in a parking lot on Ninth Avenue. Then, after 7:00 p.m., we moved the cars closer to the club to avoid the unsafe walk to Ninth Avenue at 5:00 a.m. when we finished work. We were just being smart. But you know folks—they love to talk! And the gossip actually helped, because it made people curious enough to visit Justine's to investigate, which they did. Who would have thought two sport cars would cause that much positive hype!

The CART Indy races, which Norman and I have been attending since 1985, now grew into Formula One worldwide racing

Harold attempting to ride Ed Douglas' beautiful bike at Manhattan Proper Café

Kayaking in Thimble Islands Lakes in Connecticut

Spectator Sports: The New York Mets and the New York Giants

In the 1960s and '70s, most of the kids living in Queens were New York Mets fans, since their stadium was visible in our community. Ever since the Brooklyn Dodgers left for Los Angeles in 1957, we waited patiently for a new National League team to come to the New York area. In 1962, here came the NY Mets! Despite their many initial losses in the Big Apple, we rooted for them faithfully right up to their World Series win in 1969.

Of course, one of the few Black players, Willie Mays, was our hero. He was on the San Francisco Giants team in the '60s, but whenever they played against the Mets, this heightened the excitement of attending the ballgames; and our excitement grew even more when Mays was recruited to New York to play for the Mets in the 1970s.

Mets game – September 2018

Our parents knew how to keep us busy. And when we were lucky, we saw a live game. Our godfather Princeton Sims, who lived in Washington, DC, was a huge New York Yankee fan. Every time the Yankees were in the World Series, he would drive his Lincoln Continental (he worked for the company) up to New York and take us to the game. Being Mets fans, we received absolute instructions *not* to wear any Mets gear to Yankee Stadium in the Bronx. It was a running joke that we not-so-secretly wore Mets gear underneath our outer clothing.

We also were football fans, although our mother was not a fan of us playing football. "No way, no how," she insisted, no matter what our father said. She was very concerned about injuries. So, we would cheer for our favorite players instead.

In 1981, when linebacker Lawrence Taylor joined the New York Giants' defensive line, we really had a reason to cheer. The Giants were always number one in our house. With Super Bowl championships in 1989, 1991, 2008 and 2012, they were the toast of the town. The NY Jets were in their rear-view mirror, with only one championship in 1969 when the legendary quarterback Joe Namath played for the team.

Funny, when we turned to skiing after bowling and tennis, Mom never had any notion about how dangerous skiing could be, due to the lack of coverage on American TV. The steep trails, the nosebleed chairlifts, and the crazed snowboarders whose peripheral vision was technically blinded on the left side. All this to say, just be careful out there: danger is lurking!

St. John's University photo assignment of Harold Dow at LaBelle's concert at Queens College including Sarah Dash & Nona Hendryx in the early 70s.

CHAPTER SEVEN

Friends & Lovers

Beautiful Message Songs

"As" by Stevie Wonder

"Love's in Need of Love Today" by Stevie Wonder

"Somebody Loves You Baby (You Know Who It Is)" by Patti LaBelle

---

This memoir would not be complete if it didn't pay homage to all the friends and lovers who we met over the years, and who met each other at The Dow Twins affairs. Many folks fell in love, got married, or just became great lifelong friends; and although neither Norman nor I ever married or had children ourselves (families would have been a stretch, to say the least, given our round-the-clock work schedules), we were no exceptions. This chapter is dedicated to our love stories, and to those of our many friends, written in their own words. Thanks to you all!

Love and The Dow Twins

When it came to meeting women, Norman and I started out as total novices. Thanks to our mother, we had very limited exposure to the opposite sex in our formative years. After St. Catherine's elementary school, our teen years were spent at a gender-segregated high school surrounded by graveyards and miles away from any Black girls that we might have met in our own neighborhood of Jamaica, Queens.

My mother, who was very involved with our education, sent us damn-near to Brooklyn to the newly-opened Christ the King High School in the mostly-white neighborhood of Middle Village, Queens. She chose this over Andrew Jackson High School in our neighborhood, where we wanted to attend with our friends from the block; and where we would have had the opportunity to meet girls and mature into the natural rhythm of dating.

At Christ the King, boys were separated from girls even at lunch. The Boys' Dean of Discipline, Brother Simon, was no joke, and he made sure the sexes stayed separate (and did I mention that there were only eight Black students in the incoming class of 1965?). Not until our senior year did Christ the King make the lunchroom coed, but even then, we were not especially interested in dating non-Blacks or attending their parties; that wasn't in our DNA.

It wasn't until we got to St. John's University that we had a chance to be around our female peers. Confidence with the ladies came easily for Norman, who had the "gift of gab"; but for me it was different, as I was always more reserved. By the time we were managing Justine's, however, not long after finishing college, we both had at least some dating experience under our belts.

For obvious reasons, Norman and I had a philosophy—never mix business with pleasure (although Norman sometimes had trouble following the rule—smile). We preferred for the women we dated not to hang out at our clubs or attend our events, since these were essentially our workplaces. This helped to eliminate any unnecessary drama.

It's a common problem in a business that involves singles mixing and mingling in social situations like bars and nightclubs—the coordinators of said events are likely to be the focus of a lot of attention, whether intended or not. I tried to keep my interactions with the ladies very professional by being friendly, but never too flirtatious. But this was a new experience for both of us when we were starting out. We had only become socially active in college and were still a little green when it came to the ladies.

The women of The Dow Twins! Not much controversy here, as they've been very respectful. They never wanted to mix business with pleasure. However, I can recall two or three situations where two or three very nice ladies would fortuitously find themselves still in the club at closing time and join us for breakfast.

Ray James

Our desire to keep business and pleasure separate was actually less about a policy than about a reflection of our respect for women and for our business. We realized that most of our event ticket sales and club patronage came from the ladies—so, it was important to be respectful of our female followers. We even kept the ladies in mind when deciding on the locations of our venues before booking them. We chose dates and times (as well as elegant sites with parking and accessibility) to guarantee favorable responses from our female patrons, not to mention their moms and aunts.

We were also committed to treating the women in our personal lives with respect. We had been advised by our older mentors that, by being decent to the women we dated, our female patrons would see this and realize that we were not "Playboys"—a reputation we wanted to avoid. Plus, we were brought up as good Catholic boys by the nuns (smile!), so reverence for women was second nature to us.

In fact, once while rushing up the grand staircase at the Metropolitan Museum of Art to attend The Candace Award fundraiser, I noticed an older woman in front of me managing the imposing staircase alone. Automatically, I took hold of her arm and offered to escort her to her seat. She turned and smiled gratefully and said, "Thank you, young man." At that moment, I realized that it was Coretta Scott King—all alone and unescorted. As I walked her inside, all eyes were on us, as if we were in a procession. Mrs. King should never have been left alone like this. All women, but especially our elders, need our respect and care.

Our regard for women, I am sure, also had a lot to do with our upbringing at home. Our parents always showed mutual respect. The kindness with which my father treated my mother and her mother was our example from childhood. Mom and dad had disagreements, of course, but they were always civil, even in the most difficult moments; we never heard any disrespectful arguments between them. They weren't perfect, but they were very considerate. So, it was easy to follow in their footsteps and respect our female friends, partners and patrons.

Norman

Norman and I also had different taste in women, which was beneficial to both of us, because it prevented sibling rivalries. There was never any competition, jealousy or awkward situations between us. All that being said, it was no secret that Norman was a magnet for lovely women…

> All the women loved Norman. He was designed to made women feel better—feel that they were special. He helped every woman he dated to excel, especially in their careers: a better job, a promotion. That's one of the reasons why, when he passed, all the women he had dated over the years wanted to know from me, "How did Norman really feel about me?"
>
> ❦
>
> Justice Vasquez

> Norman will always have a very special place in my heart. He convinced me to get my real estate license, and he liked to share information on life, because everyone's journey is different. He may be gone, but he will never be forgotten.
>
> ❦
>
> Virgie Baptiste

As Norman's best friend for decades, Justice Vasquez was the true witness to his love life. She knew, liked, and became close to his girlfriends, often remaining so for long after they stopped dating Norman. Justice was an understanding and caring friend to Norman's ladies and, knowing how many women were attracted to him, she did what she could to be supportive of their relationships with Norman: to comfort them when things went wrong; and, occasionally, to run interference between them, sometimes to hilarious results.

What follows are the recollections of JUSTICE, judiciously edited and paraphrased to protect the innocent (smile).

As anyone who knew Norman can vouch, he was a ladies' man—but not in the typical sense. He was especially attracted to women he could help—with career or financial advice, life circumstances, work promotions, even with their exes—whatever they needed. He elevated the women he knew by encouraging them to improve their lives; and he did whatever he could to buoy them up.

Norman made women feel good even when they were making bad decisions. He would make them feel good about themselves, their relationship, their mistakes; and he liked to feel needed. For instance, if a girlfriend called him multiple times a day—something that might irritate another man—he didn't mind at all. He would make himself available. Harold did mind, however, since the constant phone calls tended to interfere with The Twins' workday.

The influx of ladies into and out of Norman's life affected The Twins' home lives, too. Once, when they were living in their New Jersey duplex, Norman's then-girlfriend, who was a smoker, was visiting for the weekend. Even though smoking was not allowed in The Twins' home, while Norman was asleep and Harold was working his lady lit up a cigarette.

When Harold arrived home after a long night working, he could smell smoke everywhere and was not pleased. He demanded in a booming voice to know who was smoking in his house as he searched for the culprit. Norman's girlfriend was so cowed that she stayed hidden in Norman's room, afraid to reveal herself.

Norman woke at the commotion and did his best to calm Harold down enough for his lady to come out of his bedroom. She admitted to smoking and apologized. Harold said, "There's no need to apologize, just don't smoke in here again."

To which she replied, defensively, "Well, you don't live here by yourself. Norman lives here, too!" Needless to say, this was not a remark that endeared her to Harold, and it was one of many times when Norman's dating life affected his brother's tranquility. However, she never smoked in their house again!

Harold wasn't the only one who had to deal with Norman's girlfriends. I did too, especially since I was the only one who knew when Norman was dating multiple women—a frequent occurrence, although in Norman's mind he believed he ended every relationship before starting a new one. The problem was that his exes didn't always get the message because Norman preferred not to officially break up (too much drama), but rather to let each relationship "fade away" in its own time.

On one occasion, a friend of mine (and ex-girlfriend of Norman's) organized a girls' weekend at her place in Manhattan. The five women in attendance had all met each other at Othello but none realized that, except for me, they'd each dated Norman at one time or another.

When I arrived for the weekend, I was faced with four of Norman's ex-girlfriends, and I panicked. Always protective of both Norman and of the feelings of his ladies, I knew that if the group started talking about Norman, they'd find out things about him that he would not want them to know (overlapping dating timelines, for instance); and they'd likely be angry with me, too, for keeping Norman's indiscretions a secret.

I immediately set up ground rules for the weekend, and the most important one was—no talking about men! I convinced the group of ladies that the weekend should only be about us and our lives, not about men. It was the only thing I could think of to prevent a small war. There I was, stuck with four of Norman's exes for the whole weekend as I tried frantically to steer their conversations away from him.

Despite the fact that it was nearly impossible to keep the four other women from talking about men for two days, I did my best. All the while I was thinking, "Norman, I'm gonna kill you!" because it was his "fade away" break up philosophy that had gotten me into the situation. By avoiding outright breakups, Norman always left the proverbial door open, which caused problems like ex-girlfriends not knowing their "ex" status (needless to say, this was before Facebook and dating sites that list your status). Anyway, I just barely survived that weekend intact.

Norman simply had no clear boundaries when it came to his relationships. He impulsively did whatever he felt like doing, and I often seemed to find myself in the middle whenever something went wrong. In fact, most of the time, Norman didn't feel like he was doing anything wrong.

Despite sometimes driving me crazy, Norman was also one of the kindest and sweetest people I knew. He made a huge a difference in my life; and not having him around after his death made an equally big a difference. He was a surrogate brother to me, as I'd lost my own brother when I was young. Norman would often ask my advice about how to make this or that girlfriend happy; and he was quick to act on whatever ideas I had.

As I recall, one of Norman's lady friends had an adorable daughter who wanted a Barbie dreamhouse for Christmas. The mom had regretfully told her daughter, "I wish I could, but I can't afford to buy you that. Maybe next year." She told me how disappointed her daughter had been, and I shared this with Norman, suggesting that he buy the dreamhouse for his girlfriend's daughter.

At first, Norman wasn't keen on the idea, especially when I explained that he'd have to assemble the dollhouse.

"Put it together?! I don't know anything about a Barbie dreamhouse," he told me; but he couldn't resist the idea of making his girlfriend and her daughter happy. Soon enough, we were driving to EJ Korvette's department store to buy it.

Then, on Christmas Eve, we set ourselves up in the hallway outside of his girlfriend's apartment (to keep the doll house a secret from her daughter) and assembled it.

I thought that Norman's determination to make their Christmas special was so touching. But that's how sweet he was to the people he cared about. That was my brother. I even teared up a little as we maneuvered the enormous doll house into the apartment and left it by the door with a stocking that read, "Merry Christmas."

While Norman was still in his early thirties, he had another relationship with a lady who lived in a lovely, comfortable apartment. As their relationship progressed, Norman began spending a lot of time there. In fact, he practically moved in, eating and sleeping there, and even spending most days working there, doing his paperwork and making phone calls.

One day, his lady mentioned to me that her grocery, phone, and utility bills were on the rise due to Norman's constant presence in her apartment. When I asked, "Why don't you talk to him about it?" his girlfriend was reluctant and said she would feel uncomfortable mentioning it to Norman herself.

I knew what that meant: it would fall to me to alert Norman to the problem. So I did, advising him to start contributing to household costs. He was surprised. The thought hadn't occurred to him. He asked me, "Really? Did she tell you this?"

I prudently lied and said, "No, she wouldn't do that; but still, paying your way is just the right thing to do."

Norman was immediately concerned. "Oh, Wow. Do you think she's upset with me?"

"No," I assured him. "But I'm sure she would be happy if you left a few dollars with her at the end of the month, to help out." Norman's lady knew that I had advised him on the right thing do, and she thanked me later.

This particular girlfriend was very good for Norman. She taught him how a relationship was supposed to work between a man and a woman—the responsibilities, not just the fun. She also encouraged him to focus more on the details of his businesses and made him aware of areas that needed improvement work-wise.

That's when Norman really became more business-focused, like Harold, and he concentrated his efforts on his "baby"—Manhattan Proper Café ("The Proper"), where he and Harold had at last become owners rather than freelance contractors. Norman spent most of his time at The Proper—more so than Harold, who concentrated on marketing and "pop-up" events.

The Proper was good for Norman in many ways. One (debatably good) way was that it gave him access to lots of women. Among them was a lady who would turn out to be the love of his life, albeit equivocally. Her name, for the purposes of this memoir, was Lena. She had a sweet and giving personality, very much like Norman's, and she worshipped the ground he walked on. She always put Norman's needs before her own; she was always doing nice things for him; and she hung on his every word—although this was probably naive of her in my estimation.

At the time that he and Lena were dating, Norman was also seeing another lady with whom he spent Sundays by the pool at The Twins' condo complex. To keep the ladies from bumping into each other, Norman told Lena that Sunday was football day—his day off—and he preferred to spend it alone. It was unbelievable to me that Lena accepted this deception as truth, but she was very much blinded by her love for Norman … at least at first.

One Saturday night, Lena telephoned me and said, "I think I'm going to surprise Norman in the morning and visit him at home. We can spend the day watching football." This plan, if carried out, meant that two of Norman's girlfriends would meet face-to-face. I could only imagine the fall out.

Caught in the middle, yet again, I told Lena, "No! You shouldn't do that." When Lena asked why, I improvised. "Well, he'll just be getting home from The Proper at 5:00 a.m. and he'll be exhausted. That's not a good time to surprise him." But Lena would not be dissuaded. "I'm going anyway," she insisted.

Thinking fast, I invited myself along, hoping that, by being there, I could somehow avert disaster. I said, "Well, if you insist, at least let me go with you. He'll be less upset if he sees me there too. Why don't you pick me up. I'll cook, and we'll make day of it."

Lena agreed. I hung up the phone and started calling Norman immediately; but he wasn't picking up. Frantic, I called Harold, who told me that Norman was on the tennis court with his other girlfriend.

"Harold, please go and tell him to call me right away. It's an emergency."

Harold did and finally Norman phoned. When I explained the situation Norman, not surprisingly, blamed me. Again!

"How could you let this happen?" He accused me.

"I tried to stop her, but she was determined." I said, trying to defend myself.

Well, Norman had no intention of letting this scenario play out, so he said he was going to leave—take his date out to eat or something; anything to get her away from his place before Lena showed up.

When Lena arrived at my apartment to pick me up, I told her that I'd called Norman and blown the surprise; and that he was upset and did not want company.

"How could he be upset that you're coming over?" Lena asked, knowing that Norman and I were like two peas in a pod.

I made something up. "Well, it's because I don't normally come over on Sunday." Then I convinced Lena to cancel her plans and to hang out with me instead.

Lena then admitted that she suspected Norman. "Do you think he has somebody else there?" she asked.

Covering for Norman again, I said, "No! It's just that he worked three straight days and he's tired."

Love ... breakup ... makeup. That was the nature of Norman's relationship with Lena—it was very, very complicated. On the one hand, he truly loved her, and had even become close with her son, whom he cared for very much. On the other hand, he had a passion for the ladies and a history of multi-dating, to put it mildly.

But the roller coaster nature of their love affair took its toll on Lena. Over time, and after finding out through the workplace rumor mill that Norman was seeing someone else who worked at the same place she did, Lena decided to leave New York and Norman for good.

I was very hurt when Lena told me she was leaving, because we had become good friends. I remember sitting in Lena's car in a McDonald's parking when Lena broke the news. I tried to convince Lena to stay in New York and to be strong enough to let go of Norman without moving away, but Lena didn't feel that was possible. Norman had a way of making her feel wonderful and special. Giving that up was going to be hard enough from a distance, and impossible from closeby because Norman kept coming around to see her—keeping the door open. Lena's love for Norman made the pain of knowing he was dating others a crushing weight to bear.

Despite my appeals, Lena was determined to leave the city and move to Florida where she had family. The two of us cried together and for the umpteenth time, I thought, "I'm gonna kill him!" because this time Norman had cost me a friend.

I was (although I shouldn't have been) surprised to learn later that Norman hadn't been able to give Lena up. After she moved to Florida, he began to visit her there. He used

The Dow Twins group excursions to West Palm Beach as a cover, and he'd detour to visit her before returning home to New York. Meanwhile, whenever Lena visited New York to see friends and family, she also saw Norman.

Soon enough, the two were a couple again. At first they kept it a secret from me (and most everyone else, including Harold), but on one of Lena's visits to New York she asked me if she could stay with me. I was living in Manhattan at the time and was happy to put her up.

One evening, Lena told me that she was going out. When I asked where, I received only a vague answer. "Oh, just out to dinner with some friends," Lena told me and left.

A while later, I received what I thought was an unrelated phone call from Norman. He'd broken his key in his car door and needed me to bring him my spare key. When I asked where he was, I was surprised to learn that he was parked very near my apartment on Second Avenue.

As I came around the corner, I saw him standing with Lena. "What are you doing here?" I asked, and the couple burst out laughing. That's when I realized they were still together.

Norman and Lena never really broke up, but their ongoing relationship wasn't widely known. So much so that, on the day of Norman's funeral, I had to explain to Harold that Lena should be included in the services as a member of the intimate family—that she should ride in the limousine with the funeral procession and sit with the family during the ceremony.

Harold understood completely and told me not to worry.

My friend Nicole and her mom,
plus Norman's friend Sharmayne with Aunt Toni

Harold was the kindest he could be to Lena, making sure that she was treated like family. He handled everything and I was very moved and proud of him because I knew that dealing with Norman's women friends was not his favorite thing to do.

Even in death, Norman's irresistibility to women was evident. I remember holding court in Mrs. Dow's bedroom during the wake with all of Norman's ex-girlfriends in attendance. All were heartbroken and devastated, but none seemed to mind that he'd known them all. In this moment of great sorrow, they took comfort in each other.

Nevertheless, it seems that Lena was truly the love of his life. After his passing, I found items among his effects suggesting that he and Lena were planning to become engaged and that Norman might even have intended to move to Florida to live with her. Due to his tragic and untimely passing, his intentions will never be known for sure.

As told by Justice Vasquez

Harold

As for me, I have been blessed to have had some (if not as many as my brother) very special relationships in my life...

Over forty years ago, I walked into a hot nightclub called Justine's intending to hang out a bit for a couple of drinks and a simple after-work wind down with friends. Little did I know this would start me on a course that would change my life and bring so much fun, adventure, career change and, most importantly, extended family that I still love, laugh with, share with, support and enjoy to this day. We hold each other down. We lift each other up. We have history. We have crazy stories that never get old. We have a bond that has withstood, and deepened, through the passage of time. We also know the juicy inside scoop on where all the bodies are buried, so to speak (lol). But I digress...

So, I'm sitting at the bar, minding my own business, when a suave, handsome gentleman approaches and offers to buy me a drink. Well, you know, one thing leads to another, and he invites me out. We did that back then. In person. Not by text. Anyway, I gave him my number and we made a plan to meet for a first date.

My friend, who'd been watching us, said, "Do you know who that is? Well, his name is Harold Dow."

"So?" I shrugged.

"Well, Harold and Norman Dow run this club; they are big time promoters, and they do all these parties and special events…"

Well, okay. So now I feel like I've got to bring my A-game on this first big date, which was a major-sponsored Bike Ride and Picnic Event in Central Park. A bike ride? First, I don't have no damn bike and second, I'm tryin' to look grown and sexy, which means heels and a dress. I told Harold I didn't have a bike, except for my old purple kids' bike with a sparkly banana seat and streamers from the handlebars that my mom had kept in storage. I thought that would squash that. But it didn't.

So, I put together this romantic picnic basket of Cornish game hens, cheese, fruit, champagne … you get the picture. Harold shows up to my house and loads that purple freakin' bike onto his car. I'm like, "You're not serious." He was.

We show up to Justine's and there are bikers in neoprene and helmets assembling their bikes! Well, here I am (with my petite self), pedaling furiously, dodging traffic through the city streets behind all these serious bikers, trying to keep up on my sparkly banana seat bike.

People are like, "Who is that little girl on that bike behind Harold?" Everybody was laughing their asses off. Thus was my less-than-auspicious introduction to the wonderful world of The Dow Twins and TBOF.

I was pissed. But I got over it and had to laugh at myself. And in so doing, I got some street cred and some good sport points that stood me in good stead for the rest of my forty-plus year relationship with this crew. Wouldn't change a thing. Eventually, Harold and I decided we were better as friends than boyfriend and girlfriend. We were and still are.

༺

Dawne Steward Walton

Another special woman in my life was introduced to me by our bartender and friend, Lee Robinson. She set us up when she held her wedding reception at our restaurant, The Proper Café, in 1990. Lee arranged for her girlfriend's daughter, Natalie, to be seated with me and my mom—and that's all she wrote. Natalie and I were an instant hit, and later that evening I found myself offering to escort her home—on public transportation, no less!

Harold Dow with girlfriend Natalie Hurdle

As I took the #5 train to the last stop in the

Bronx where she lived, I wondered what I was doing way up there in no man's land (which the Bronx was at the time). I was enjoying her company, that's what. I walked four blocks up to her building and dropped her home safely. On my way back down the hill to the subway, I walked on the double yellow lines in the middle of the street (the streetwise know this tactic to avoid being mugged in a dark alley). It was dark and my senses said, "You don't know this neighborhood; be alert." But the multi-hour-roundtrip late night journey was worth it.

Natalie and I dated happily for a couple of years. After that, she was offered a deal she couldn't refuse on a great house just minutes from Philadelphia. When she moved, my thought was, "This isn't going to work out because, between my busy schedule and the hazards of driving in a luxury car down on the NJ turnpike (where state troopers loved to pull over people of color), the long-distance nature of the relationship is going to be a problem." So, we decided to take a time out and, later, we moved on.

Natalie and Harold having fun in the Poconos Resorts, New Jersey

We remained good friends, though; and when Natalie married in 1994, I attended her wedding. The next thing I knew, her mom called to say, "Your girl is pregnant—with twins!" Which, ironically, Natalie once thought she was going to have with me. Although her marriage ended after only two years, she did have the twins, and her mom and dad were there to help her out.

At the time of the birth of Natalie's twin sons, Norman and I promised that if they attended college, they would receive the scholarship award we had funded in our father's name. When, years later, they did enroll at university, we kept our promise. Her mom and her older daughter Sherri Ann accepted the awards on behalf of the boys, who had already started their life journeys as freshman at the HBCU Lincoln University in Pennsylvania.

Even before this, in 2000, Natalie and I had started dating again. She would come up to New York on the weekends after her ex picked up the twins (usually late—which made her late arriving in New York—but I was just happy to see her). Although our time together was often limited to weekends, it was priceless anyway. We dated for ten years. We had fun traveling to the Poconos, Orlando, and other weekend getaways until, much to our dismay, Natalie was diagnosed with a rare form of cancer, and it didn't go well. She suffered through the various cancer stages that followed and, sadly, passed away in January of 2020 at fifty-eight years young. She will always be missed.

Les Amies

Throughout our lives and careers, there were a few special women friends (Justice Vasquez and Dawne Steward Walton, especially) who, though not lovers, were equally important to us. Not only did we work together, but we played together and stayed friends for life. Based upon their stories, we meant the same to them.

I thank God for Norman and Harold coming into my life. I had a forty-two-year relationship that was all positive, and it changed my life forever ... In the nightclub business there are temptations—you could drink, get high ... but The Twins never allowed me to do anything like that, and I became their little sister. They'd say, "You're not dating customers," and tell me who I was going to date. We spent so much time together.

I was especially close to Norman. He was a saint to me. God gives you angels, and he was my angel. He taught me as much as he could teach me. He directed me as much as he could direct me, and he talked me to death (smile). Norman loved well and was able to accept love. It would feel so good when he would introduce me as his little sister.

Norman and I had only one disagreement over a lifetime of friendship. Once while we were in the kitchen at The Proper Café, I overheard him on the phone speaking harshly to his mom about something minor, and it bothered me. I told him, "I'm not gonna speak to you until you apologize to your mother." For five days I was so miserable. You would have thought my boyfriend had dumped me. I missed him talking to me. We worked together for those few days, but we wouldn't speak to each other. After five days, he came to me and gave me a big hug. I said, "I missed you."

Harold, on the other hand, never liked "mushy." If you were openly affectionate with him, he might shy away. Once I phoned him and said, "Good afternoon, brother."

He responded "Justice, I like my name." In other words, he did not want me to refer to him as my "brother." I was hurt at first, but then realized that was just Harold's way. He was uncomfortable accepting overt expressions of love. But I knew (and still know) in my heart that if I ever needed Harold, he was going to be there for me.

In fact, he paid for my wedding in 2018 and never even told me (to avoid a big hug and kiss, I guess). I didn't know this until after the fact. He told everyone, "I don't care what she wants, let her have whatever it is. Don't let her choose something less to save money."

Harold is like that with everyone, not just me. With all the things that he's been through and all his losses and medical problems, God has blessed him with life and health. God is keeping him here for a reason. There are people who love him very much, including me—his "sister."

ॐ

Justice Vasquez

You cannot talk about The Dow Twins without Justice—'JV.' They were a triumvirate. Worked together. Played together. These three were ride or die family. And somehow, in a most unlikely scenario, I became a sort of fourth wheel and got to know and become close with each of these unique characters.

By my second date with Harold, it became clear that I was gonna need to be tested, approved and blessed by Justice if our relationship had any chance of going anywhere.

Justice of the Fendi bags, fur coats, and Dom Pérignon. She was a diva ... the "queen bee" of Justine's. And The Twins loved her. I made up my mind she was gonna like me. And she did...

There are so many stories to be told about my times with TBOF and The Dow Twins, but some of the most memorable revolve around our efforts to create special and, admittedly over the top, celebrations for our friends.

The thing was, being in the nightclub business, we were so out of sync with almost everybody else. We did not do nine-to-five. And so, our social circle was comprised of all the people we worked with, really liked hanging out with and who, because of our mutual schedules, could hang out with us.

And, of course, many of our high-profile clients had money (legally obtained or otherwise—smile) and flashed it freely in the clubs on Dom Pérignon with a straw. The ones that didn't have bucks tried to look like they did. But the super successful TBOF and Dows were seriously banking legit Benjamins hand over fist. Not me, of course. I was mostly broke. But my friends always had my back, and I was in the inner circle, so to speak, so of course I also enjoyed my fair share of special birthday parties (I think one involved me being pushed out into the crowd in a straw skirt and coconut bra).

Once I was able to surprise the normally-nosey and impossible-to-surprise Justice with a private sunset yacht party around New York for her birthday. The gleaming ship was impressive with first class luxury on every deck.

Mami Carmen provided her famous pernil and rice and gandules dish, and the caterers laid on the rest of the gourmet spread. I made the boys provide every conceivable type of baller drink aboard. The music was pumping, the view gorgeous, and all her friends came in from out of town. It was gooood.

But the time that stands out the most—the time Justice and I laugh about at least once a year—was the time we were immortalized forevermore as the "helicopter people." Now, normally Justice and I were partners-in-crime party planners. The thing was, we'd set the bar so high that each time we had to outdo whatever had been done before. And at this point, even with money, that wasn't easy.

So, we decided to do something different for the Dow's Birthday that year. No party. No crowd. Something more intimate with just me, Justice, Harold and Norman. Just us. But it had to be good. So, we came up with the idea of a private helicopter tour of New York and then dinner. However, we had to find a restaurant where the helicopter could land. After much research we found one and made the reservation. Afterwards, we planned for a stretch limo to pick us up from the restaurant and take us to the Playboy Club (hey, it was the eighties ya'll).

So, part one: we surprise the boys with the helicopter ride and land in front of the restaurant. It was like Mission Impossible. People came running out to greet us and escort us into the restaurant. From the concierge to the servers, everyone kept asking us all night "are you the helicopter people?"

Flinging our hair appropriately, Justice and I were like "Yes, that would be us." I don't even remember what we ate, but I know we owned the room and got the red-carpet treatment till we signed the check and got into our awaiting stretch limo with champagne on ice en route to the Playboy Club.

Now we're in the limo on our way, and me and Justice try and get Norman and Harold to smoke this joint with us. Okay stop it! Don't judge us (again, it was the eighties ya'll). In those days, everybody smoked a little weed. Everybody except The Dow Twins. These guys were boy scouts in a den of iniquity that was the club scene. They didn't drink much and definitely didn't do drugs of any kind. Harold wanted to be able to count money, and Norman wanted to be able to get lucky. But we begged and cajoled until Norman eventually gave in and took one baby toke. Victory!

Well, we had a fabulous time dancing, drinking and laughing at the Playboy Club and, hours later, on the ride home. Maybe the best ever.

Dawne Steward Walton

When speaking of lifelong women friends, I must talk about Romney Williams, our first graphic artist. We laughed recently as we celebrated her (I can't believe) seventieth birthday on Mother's Day 2023. We can't even remember how we met back in the early 1970s and became such fast friends, but it doesn't matter. Romney was a Parson's School of Design student when we met, and we would stay late into the night to design promotional flyers with her illustrations, usually for printing the next day.

This went on until she graduated and became a successful runway model in Europe for years. Our friendship remained even after she had a son and through a twenty-five-year marriage to a popular (Bruce Springsteen type) European singer. The love and affection never wavered over five decades; and even now she looks fifty and can still party with the best of the young folks. Thank you again for helping Norman and I start our five-decade adventure of "Bringing People Together."

Romney Williams

I Met My Spouse at a Dow Twins' Event

One of our key responsibilities as party hosts was to make sure everyone had fun, especially the wall flowers. One strategy we used to get the shy guys to mix and mingle was to introduce them to the women we were chatting with and then excuse ourselves in the middle of a conversation, leaving them alone to carry on. It worked well, and it gave the ladies someone to dance and party with.

While we had a large female following right from the start, we had to cultivate male followers as well. It was vital to our success and to that of our clubs that we associate ourselves with male-centered organizations, and so we did. As a result of our matchmaking efforts, many marriages and friendships ensued after being sparked at a Dow Twins' event.

THE DOW TWINS' LEGACY

I met Harold & Norman Dow in 1968. I would always hear about The Dow Twins' parties. After meeting The Twins in person, we became good friends, and they put me on their mailing list; that was the mailing list you wanted to be on. I was trying to get my life together after returning from Vietnam: attending college and finding a good job. I didn't miss a Dow Twins function. They were great places to network and meet some great friends that I have till today.

I met my first wife through friends of The Twins when she was attending Hunter College to become a teacher. Most of the friends I have today, I met through The Dow Twins: that's over fifty years. Although some of our friends and family have passed on, like Norman, I still consider Harold and Norman family. God Bless,

Jim Dingle
Valued friend and patron

As a single young woman, I frequented many of the clubs/events that The Dow Twins were associated with. These venues were a place where Black Americans could go to meet other Blacks who were on the come-up. Each and every venue was special, with its own distinct vibe. There was something happening every night of the week.

But I was one of the lucky ones that met the love of my life at Justine's on a Tuesday night. My friend Cynthia and I were out having drinks when Hollis Copeland and Geoff

Houston came into the club. They both played basketball for the New York Knicks. We started talking, and I asked if he had a pro affiliation. He said yes, and I rolled my eyes with disdain.

Hollis asked for my number, and I said, "No, you're not going to walk around this club, collect a bunch of numbers, and not know who you're calling tomorrow." After that, he never left my side! We've been married forty years!

Delene Copeland

As you might expect, Hollis has a slightly different memory of their meeting:

I used to frequent Justine's, Leviticus, Red Parrott, and The Copa back in the day with Michael Ray Richardson, Ray Williams, Geoff Huston, Mike Glenn, Sly Williams, Earl Monroe, Cheese Johnson, Mike Gaye, Walt Frazier and Reggie Carter (deceased) just to name a few. Radio celebrities Vaughn Harper and Frankie Crocker would join us, and we'd all have a ball after Knick games.

In the summer of 1980, after practicing with Dean Meminger and Geoff Huston at Hudson Gill gym, Geoff and I decided to hang out at Justine's, and we saw these very attractive ladies drinking champagne. We had to make their acquaintances as quickly as possible, so we offered them a drink. In return, they invited us to sit and drink champagne with them.

I had to perform at a basketball clinic early the next morning and asked for Delene's phone number. She replied, "Only if you stay with us here the rest of the night." The rest is history. Delene and I, with Cynthia Monell and George Harris, would double date most weekends at either Justine's or Leviticus. Great times; great memories. We've been married forty years now, with two children—Yasmin, forty, and Julian, thirty years old.

Hollis Copeland

Norman and I were so fortunate to have fostered many longtime relationships and friendships with New York Knicks team members who attended our events over five decades, including Hollis.

Marko, Melissa and "Soul Fixin'" Eric

FRIENDS & LOVERS

Among the many spouses who met at one of our clubs or events are Marko Nobles, who met his wife Melissa in 1999 at one of our Manhattan Center events; Millie Garcia and Julius Williams, who met at Justine's on a Salsa Friday; Eric Reape, who met his wife Edna at The Proper Café; and Jimmy Bryant, who met his wife Keisha at a Dow Twins event at the Copacabana, as Keisha remembers well (although Jimmy remembers differently):

The night I met Jimmie:

I was invited to The Dow Twins' MASKquerade party at the Copacabana by my god-sister Donna Martinez in November 2003. Her cousin Marko (Nobles), who worked with radio station WWRL, was selling tickets to the event. Donna purchased the tickets weeks before the party, but when the night finally came, I wasn't up for it. I was suffering from severe cramps and PMS was not being very nice to me. I called Donna to tell her that I was not up to going to the party and she flipped. She said, "I brought you a ticket and was looking forward to us hanging out; you can't back out on me!" I gave in and went to the party feeling miserable and bloated.

When I got there, I was offered drinks by a few gentlemen, which was surprising because I didn't feel like my best self. After a few drinks, I felt much better and began to enjoy myself. I was in a corner acting silly with my friends doing the robot to "Dancing Machine" by the Jackson 5 and over walked a handsome, tall, well-dressed man to offer me a drink. I'd really had enough drinks for the night but said yes because he seemed so nice.

He brought me an apple martini with Kettle One vodka and walked away. He didn't ask me to dance or try to hang around, which is something most men do after buying a woman a drink. This piqued my interest. I asked him, "Where are you going? Don't you want to dance?"

He said, "Sure, but I can't dance to calypso music," which was playing at that moment. I said, "Don't worry, I'll teach you."

We danced a few records; then he said thank you and walked away. Again, my interest was piqued because he didn't try to stick around or ask for my number.

About ten minutes later, he came back with his number written on a napkin. He said, "Here is my number. Call me if you want," and walked away a third time. I felt that he was interesting, fine—and arrogant! I waited three weeks to call him (of course, I had to make this arrogant gentleman wait—there was no way I was coming off fast or desperate), and the rest is history.

Jimmie and I will have been together twenty years in November 2023 and married eighteen years on June 27, 2023. We have a son and daughter together and live a wonderful life. He is absolutely the best thing that ever happened to me.

༄

Keisha Bryant

The night I met Keisha:

I was at a MASKquerade Ball given by my friends, The Dow Twins, at The Copacabana in early November 2003. I was standing next to my partner Ray James when I observed a woman wearing a one-piece black velour jump suit, walking across the room to get a drink at the bar. She was attractive. I then turned to Ray and said, "She looks like she lives outside of New York" which, to me, meant a less-than-ideal long-distance situation, so I lost interest and she disappeared into the crowd.

Soon enough, though, she came across the room for a second drink. I couldn't take my eyes off her. My eyes followed her to the area where her table was. At this point I decided to walk across the room to where she was doing the robot dance near her table of friends. I asked if I could buy her a drink and she said yes, and we walked to the bar where I bought her the drink.

Enjoying an evening Labor Day Weekend event with friends at Martha's Vineyard in Massachusetts

We started talking and she asked me to dance. I'm not a good dancer. A Latin record was playing, and I couldn't salsa, so she said she would lead. I said okay, and she made me look good on the dance floor. I walked her back to her table, then walked to the bar and asked the bartender for a pen and paper.

The (lady) bartender asked, "Are you taking my phone number?" I said no, but she handed me the pen and paper anyway. I said thanks and made my way back to Keisha's table. I wrote my number on the paper and told her to give me a call when she could. She then took three weeks to call me! She thought I was arrogant and wanted me to wait.

FRIENDS & LOVERS

When Keisha finally called me, she said, "I have a five-year-old daughter and we come as a package deal." We have now been married eighteen years with a son added to our family.

❧

Jimmy Bryant

This chapter, out of necessity, is the PG version of The Dow Twins and friends love stories. To know the whole truth—well, you just had to be there.

Celebrating Norman's Anniversary Awards Dinner Gala
in Three of His Favorite Venues

235

CHAPTER EIGHT
Giving Back to the Community

Hit Songs

"My Lovin' (You're Never Gonna Get It)" by En Vogue
"This Is How We Do It" by Montell Jordan
"Home" by Stephanie Mills

Due to limited visits with our neighbors, for years we thought that growing up with a mother, father, and grandmother as part of our immediate family structure was nothing unique. Our two best friends and our bowling and high school buddies all had two-parent households like us.

Not until after our father's passing, during our college years and our formative years in business, did we realize that ours wasn't the norm. Norman and I learned how many families were broken or destroyed by the Vietnam conflict, during which honest, hardworking young Black men were shipped to the front lines and killed or returned broken to what had once been a strong family structure. These were the Black Baby Boomers, and their circumstances motivated Norman and me to want to "give back" to the Black community, which was being decimated by so much economic, political and social strife at the time.

As Norman and I became more successful, we began to explore philanthropy with a purpose. With no children of our own, coupled with how we were raised, made philanthropy a no-brainer. We had learned, and changed, so much during our college years that we thought it made sense to provide college scholarships to high school graduating seniors. We had overheard a single parent talking about the happiness she felt when her daughter was accepted into college, but the cost of books was prohibitive.

With no formal foundation at first, we decided to begin our altruistic journey by helping high school seniors with the cost of textbooks for college. We accepted applications from the children, friends and relatives of our followers and, being twins ourselves, we also created a special category for twins.

Dow Scholarships

Norman and I instantly thought of honoring our father by naming the scholarships after him (and later, I re-named them after Norman). In recognition of our dad and our patrons, we established The Reginald N. Dow Memorial Scholarship. Its inaugural fundraiser was held in conjunction with our 20th Anniversary Gala at the Waldorf-Astoria Hotel in 1989. The second was hosted at the Vista Hotel at the World Trade Center in 1992; the third, at the New York Sheraton Hotel in 1995; and yet another at the Copacabana in 2000.

GIVING BACK TO THE COMMUNITY

Harold Dow presenting awards aboard the 2008 USS Intrepid Benefit Gala for Norman's Memorial Scholarship Awards for distinguished friends

In honor of my late brother, we organized the Inaugural Norman F. Dow Fundraiser aboard the USS Intrepid Museum on Saturday, December 6th, 2008. The second Norman F. Dow Fund Benefit was held a little over three years later, on October 15th, 2011 at the New York Mets' CitiField. And in 2015, the 10th Anniversary Norman Dow Fund Gala was hosted at Terrace on the Park at the old World's Fair grounds in Queens.

Over time, the awardees numbered more than thirty students, and we donated over $75,000 out of our own pockets. We were also blessed by the contributions of our dear friends, including the family of my collaborator on this memoir, the Farrington family, who donated to help these young people right up until the end of our fifth decade of entertaining in NYC.

Scholarships were awarded continuously through 2023, and among the many worthy scholarship recipients were Daria Thomas, Anika Victoria Wong, Afiya Gamble, Danielle Thomas, Rena Andrews, Janelle Simmons, Lisa Hodge, Anissa Smith, Carla Simpson, Devon Prioleau, Charles Pringle, Tiffany Jackson (now a well-established author), Jasmine J. Jones, Hunter Haymore-Berry, Kiefer and Kraig Hurdle-Wilson, Italia Parks, Justin Blythe, Billy Mullings, Brandon Donaldson, Carl Bartlett, Brianna Gaines (who became a medical doctor in 2020) and Tracey L. Hunter (who became a medical doctor in 2021).

GIVING BACK TO THE COMMUNITY

Seated in the front row: awardees with parents.
Standing: WBLS VP Charles Warfield, on-air personalities Vaughn Harper and Ken 'Spider' Webb, Dr. Anita Underwood, Patricia Hodgins, Norman Dow, Mrs. Evelyn Dow, and Harold Dow

Seated next to Mom, presenter & former Supremes' Mary Wilson at our Annual Scholarship Gala

The Farrington Family donating at the Norman F. Dow Benefit Dinner

The folks enjoying dinner and dancing at Terrace
on the Park Norman's Gala

Many guests enjoying friends at Norman's Benefit Gala
at Terrace on the Park

Norman's Benefit guests visiting the Jackie Robinson salute at NY Mets' CitiField Stadium

Supporting Non-Profits

In addition to scholarships, we offered our time, energy, connections and professional expertise to benefit many worthy organizations. One of our favorite ways to 'give back' to our community was through the Jackie Robinson Foundation's (JRF) annual "An Afternoon of Jazz." The event series (initiated by the Robinson family) was held in Stamford, Connecticut at the home of Major League Baseball great Jackie Robinson. It hosted over 500 people and raised money first for civil rights activism and later for college scholarships as well.

I was introduced to the foundation when, one year, I was invited to one of the jazz concerts by a friend, Gail Stallworth. It was such an elegant picnic setting, with a lake on the property—although, as I recall, at one point we all had to duck under a tented area to escape a short rain shower, but the concert carried on from there.

Jackie Robinson's wife Rachel, Harold Dow and
JRF President Betty Phillips Adams

Afterwards, the JRF "An Afternoon of Jazz" Executive Producer, Robin Bell Stevens, inquired if we would be interested in helping increase their attendance. Since it was a non-profit organization, we thought it might be a great way to give back and, at the same time, to expose our clientele to something new and unique. "An Afternoon of Jazz" already had a great reputation and a great line-up of artists who donated part of their performance fees by charging very reasonable rates.

GIVING BACK TO THE COMMUNITY

It didn't take long to convince our baby boomer followers to include this event in their early summer schedules. They embraced the fundraiser from day one, and it quickly became part of our annual outing line-up as an excursion to a bucolic outdoor oasis in Connecticut. The Sunday picnic setting was perfect for our friends' groups and families. We were honored to market the JRF "An Afternoon of Jazz" to our audience, and we helped raise funds and increase their attendance to nearly 8,000 people.

In subsequent seasons, the concert moved to Cranberry Park in Norwalk (and for one year it was held in Tanzania in Africa).

The Jackie Robinson Foundation's "Afternoon of Jazz" was one of the premier, "not to be missed" social events in the northeast every summer. I certainly enjoyed working with that fine, eclectic group of people that would put that event on.

Harold oversaw Audience Development. He had an extensive mailing list that could be trusted. No riffraff here! We knew what the audience was looking for and could provide exactly what they wanted. I, who was part of the jazz community like the producer Ms. Robin Bell, helped bring in artists like Terrence Blanchard, Winton Marsalis, Betty Carter and, with Norman's help, Bobby Rodriguez and many other Latin artists!

Ray James
Audience Development JRF Team Member

Norman dancing with Cynthia Moore, lead sponsor with Anheuser-Busch, as the Bobby Rodriguez Latin Band encouraged the audience to start dancing salsa in place (on their blankets)

In addition to the Jackie Robinson Foundation, other non-profit organizations that we supported included the New York Urban League, The Minisink Boys, The Urban Network, The United Negro College Fund, The Dave Winfield Foundation (with a star-studded event at Club Visage), The Negro Ensemble Company, Pathways for Youth, The Dance Theatre of Harlem, the USS Intrepid Foundation, the South Africa Mandela Project, the Hurricane Katrina Relief Fundraiser, the St. John's University Alumni Association and last, but not least, the Men Who Cook Benefit with Harlem fashion icon Lana Turner (benefiting the Harlem Children's Museum Art Fund).

GIVING BACK TO THE COMMUNITY

On Sept. 29th, 1985, we had the privilege of celebrating our mother's favorite charity, The Negro Ensemble Theatre Company's "Reach for the Stars" event, with NY Knick Bernard King and actor Denzel Washington

NY Yankee Dave Winfield presented a proclamation alongside the Twins and Bob Belle

THE DOW TWINS' LEGACY

Joined by The Dow Twins were Nick Ashford and Valerie Simpson (right) and Valerie's brother Ray

Rolanda Watts (former TV Anchorperson) says "Two Good to Be True" at the "Men Who Cook" Benefit in New York City

Chef Richard from Richard's Place, model Veronica Webb, and a happy Harold Dow from The Proper Café at the Men Who Cook affair

THE DOW TWINS' LEGACY

Since we always loved supporting worthwhile causes, "Men Who Cook" was an easy choice; and when Lana Turner invites you to participate in a men's cooking event, you just say *yes*. Each year, as the event got larger, it moved from Harlem's Riverside Church to midtown's Pier 92, and finally to the American Express Pavilion at the World Trade Center (pre-2001 attacks).

It was around the time of the opening of Manhattan Proper Café in Queens, and we were pumped up to have an opportunity to feature a dish from our new menu at the "Men Who Cook" event. The only catch was that we actually had to cook—not a Dow Twins' forte. Norman, more so than I, had a handle on it, though. Since he worked at The Proper Cafe daily, he asked Robert Gaines, our chef, to help us out, which he did. Robert prepared a great dish for the event, and the Children's Museum Art Fund benefited from the money raised.

Dow Twins Honored For Their Commitment To The Community

The Harlem Chamber of Commerce presented a community service award to "social engineers" Harold and Norman Dow (aka The Dow Twins) for their 30-year commitment of bringing people together and for giving back to the community through their participation in fundraisers for such organizations as the Jackie Robinson Foundation, the New York Urban League, and The Reginald Dow Scholarship fund. Pictured (from l to r): Stephanie Francis of Harlem Chamber of Commerce, Harold A. Down, Noel N. Hankin, VP of Corporate Affairs for Schieffelin & Somerset Co.; Norman Dow; and Voza Rivers of Voz Entertainment. Schieffelin & Somerset is the prime importer of a variety of world-renowned spirits and wines including such brands as Moet & Chandon, Hennessy, Johnnie Walker, Grand Marnier and Tanqueray. *(Photo by Allen Morgan)*

GIVING BACK TO THE COMMUNITY

The "give back" starts at home as Manhattan Proper and friends support Revlon's Walkathon against Cancer

CHAPTER NINE

Epilogue—Moving On

Spiritual Songs

"Jesus Promised Me A Home Over There" by Jennifer Hudson

"The Battle Is the Lord's" by Yolanda Adams

"I Look to You" by Whitney Houston

When Norman and I started this journey, we never knew how long it would last; and, like everyone else, we didn't know if, or when, we would get married or have children. As it turned out, we were so busy entertaining the masses with smiles on our faces that we didn't make time to create a family on our own. Our family was our friends and clientele. We had matured with them during our more than fifty-year adventure and through our many events.

Although we didn't have our own children, we did our best to uplift others and, as far as we were concerned, ours was a life well-lived—until I had time to reflect. Norman's passing made it very clear that we may have missed out on an important part of life, but I have no regrets. I'm very proud of what we created—something from practically nothing that ultimately generated so much happiness. When you start a new business like we did, you just flow with the energy until it stops. It didn't stop for us until November 10th, 2005, when Norman, asleep in our childhood home, didn't wake up.

> I remember every moment of the day Norman passed. Harold called me at 6:05 a.m. to break the news. I was tasked with calling Norman's girlfriend to tell her what had happened. After Norman had his initial heart attack on that Tuesday night at the Copa, she had made plans to fly up from Miami to be with him on Thursday. She wondered if she should fly up right away, on that same day, but Norman told me to tell her that there was no need; Thursday would be fine.
>
> Of course, Norman passed on Thursday morning before she arrived, and I knew I had to reach her before she boarded the plane to give her the sad news. When she picked up the phone, I couldn't get the words out. I stammered a few times and she suddenly realized why I was calling, especially because I (a night person) had phoned her so early in the morning.
>
> She began screaming and dropped the phone. I could hear her crying out, "God, help me." All I could do was cry. When she picked up the phone again, I asked her what time her flight got in and arranged to pick her up. It was the darkest of days.
>
> So many people came to pay their respects, we had to put a sign on Mrs. Dow's door asking them to please give us a

EPILOGUE—MOVING ON

day or two to pull ourselves together. But we couldn't stem the flow of mourners. Harold was our rock. He planned the funeral like a major event: which it was, with literally thousands of mourners. We could hardly believe the massive turnout.

Some people were upset that Bogard's (the Best of Friends Midtown East nightclub) didn't close for a few days in memoriam, but the owners, Tony Cooper and Danny Berry, felt strongly that there had to be a place for people to come and learn the details of what happened and to commiserate. There were so many posts, emails and inquiries—Norman's people literally crashed our website, DowTwins.com

Many posted of how Norman had helped them in their lives and did them favors. People in the neighborhood told stories about Norman's many kindnesses to them also. Norman had kept all of this to himself. He never talked about these things. He was very modest.

After Norman passed, Harold would call more often, and we became closer friends. I don't know if Harold shares the same connection to me as I do to him, but when my husband-to-be asked for my hand in marriage, Harold showed just how much he cared (I was surprised to be getting married for the first time at sixty years old). We married on Norman's birthday, and Harold not only gave me away but paid for the wedding. I never expected to become attached to Harold—he doesn't normally allow that—but I did, and now I always know that he's there for me.

When Norman passed, Harold reminded us all of something important—he was not Norman, and he could not replace him. I knew what he meant. As Norman's identical twin, many of Norman's people looked to Harold to fill the empty space left by his brother. Since he was mourning himself, Harold could hardly be expected to fill such a need for others. And when he said, "A lot of people might be feeling that the wrong brother died," I knew what he meant by that, too. Norman was larger than life. It was not easy being his less-outgoing brother, even though the two men were clearly equals, each in their own way.

Justice Vasquez
Friend and colleague for nearly forty-five years

After it received half-a-million hits from friends and followers checking to see if the rumors were true about Norman's untimely passing, our website did indeed crash.

The worst of it, for me, was having to tell my mother, in the next room, that her son was gone.

EPILOGUE—MOVING ON

Norman's final photo at The Copa on 34th Street with the WWRL 1600 sales team

Condolence Messages for Norman

We received so many heartfelt condolence messages, I wanted to share a few that reflect how widely-beloved my brother was. This section is a collection of those messages.

> I would like to offer my sincere regrets to Harold Dow and family on the passing of Norman. As much as we will all miss celebrating with him at the annual events, I know he's part of an even bigger celebration where he is now.
>
> We sincerely express our deepest sympathy to you and your family. As with so many others, it was a total surprise

to us when we received the call. You and your brother have always, without a doubt, been friends to Michael and me over the years. It was always a pleasure to see you guys in the summer and then to see you again on the ski mountain. We will treasure the fond memories of Norman, and will truly celebrate his life as I know he would have wanted all of us to do.

So, if we don't get to shake your hand or send a smile your way at the services (yes, we will attend), please know that our thoughts, prayers and condolences are with you and your family.

Bless you and celebrate life.

To Harold Dow, Mama Dow, and Family

Please accept my heartfelt condolences on the "early" homegoing of Norman.

I met the infamous Dow Twins in the '70s, and I have enjoyed and supported their endeavors ever since. Norman and Harold have always been nothing but professional and always gentlemen. Always!

I will miss Norman, but it will only be a "physical miss." He will always be here with us spiritually.

May God continue to bless Norman's beautiful soul, and I also ask that God continue to bless Harold and his family during the coming days and years. May God bless you forever.

Take care of yourself, Harold!

EPILOGUE—MOVING ON

Harold, I am deeply saddened to hear of your brother Norman's passing. He was a warm and wonderful person and will certainly be missed. Norman contributed so much joy and happiness to New York's Black social scene. There is no doubt The Dow Twins legacy will continue, and so will our memory of Norman.

Sincerely, G. Keith Alexander
Celebrity Radio Host

I attended Christ the King High School and remember Norman as my classmate. I offer my condolences to his family. The first time I formally met him, though, was at Manhattan Proper. My mother, Lynn Jackson, had a birthday party there, and from then on, I was hooked. Every year the Intrepid, the Copa ... my friends, family ... we all made sure that whatever we did throughout the year ... we were on that USS Intrepid.

When I heard the news, I immediately called my mother, who was saddened for more reasons than one. Fifty-five is young, and a wonderful personality had been lost to her; and so, she felt "cheated," as she had shared many great times with The Dow Twins, as did so many, many, many people. I know it's selfish to think like that, but we are all human and, in this day and age, great times are hard to come by.

Icons in your own right, may God bless you with whatever your needs are at this moment to sustain you and your family. Countless prayers for strength. But have Peace in knowing that many people pass along without feeling as if they have made a "difference" or their "mark" on the world ... this is not one of those cases. Be happy in knowing that Norman is responsible for endless smiles and great times ...

Respectfully, Mia Williamson – Daughter of Lynn Jackson
(Mt. Vernon / Montclair, NJ)
WE LOVE YOU!

I've had the pleasure of knowing Norman for at least thirty-four years. What a consistent honorable brother he is. Man, they will be throwing down in heaven. I can see him greeting people at the pearly gates with that big smile on his face.

He is loved and will be missed.

Michael

I am one of the many who share good times during the Justine's era. Mr. Norman Dow was indeed the warmest person I had ever met; although I was one of many that he shared a little time with here and there. He will be missed. Accept my deepest sympathy at this time of your pain. May God give your family the strength to continue his memory.

God Bless.

EPILOGUE—MOVING ON

Deep love, compassion, and prayers I send to the Dow Family. Because Norman was a great soul and friend who created great memories for so many, it tempers my grief of his transition. I fondly remember his smile, vision and contributions; qualities we all can pass along to honor our great friend. He achieved, in my opinion, the two greatest things in life—a personal relationship with God, and the awareness and completion of his assignment in life! Dance floors and concert halls vibrate songs for a maestro gone too soon. Rest in peace, dear friend. You sang your song to completion!

Loving you always,
Bobbi Humphrey

Just want to honor such a fine, friendly and compassionate friend whom I have enjoyed over the years. Norman will be truly missed by me and all those he has touched throughout his profession as a special event coordinator and promoter. I met Norman while operating our own events, under the name of Top Shelf Productions, Inc., back in the day. Harold, my heart goes out to you because you have lost your brother, best friend and business partner. But your new partner is God, and he will see you through these difficult times. May God bless you and your family for now and in the future.

God must want to open the ultimate club in heaven. Do you think that's why he called Norman home to put it together? I'm so at a loss for words. A mother is not supposed to bury her child. A twin is not supposed to bury his twin. I'm a mother of teenage twins so, Harold, I can only imagine your pain. Mrs. Dow and Harold, I pray that during this terrible time memories will sustain you. Luckily for you both, your sons/brother are stars, so there are lots of pictures, many stories, and great times that will keep him up close and personal.

Know that we share your loss and all who know you and knew Norman are holding our hands out to you offering help; and our arms are wide open offering you hugs and support. Thank you, Norman, for all you gave us!

I've known Norman for as long as I can remember. Justine's: what fun we used to have. I am simply shocked and saddened. Thank you for sharing him with us. A sweeter, nicer person you'll never know. And Harold, my heart goes out to you especially. I still remember coming in the club and calling you "Twin" because you always seemed to fool me. This is Deb, and you will remember me as soon as you see me. Love you, dear. I will miss him.

Deb, Bronx, NY

EPILOGUE—MOVING ON

I am so saddened by the loss of Norman. I am still in shock. We had plenty of good times together that I will forever remember. He actually made me a part of who I am today: a lady of elegance, being in their presence at clubs of such sophistication back in the '70s, '80s, '90s, etc. I don't even have any words to say; I am numb ... But I must at least say something before Norman is laid to rest.

Harold, I am so sorry, but we know that he is at peace and free from any pain, trouble or worries that he may have had at his last moments while he talked with the Lord, I am sure, in his sleep. Harold, I am not able to be there with you, because I just left Queens on November 7th after attending my aunt's funeral and cannot get back this week, but my prayers are with you. I love you and I will be there in the Spirit.

Wisteria

Harold,

Just to let you know that our deepest sympathy goes out to you and your family. Wishing you much brighter tomorrows when this difficult time has passed.

Always, Jr. and Eunice Talbot (Bermuda)

Dearest Harold and family,

I am profoundly saddened by your loss. Although I no longer reside in NY, I have such fond memories of the good times and wonderful laughs that I shared with Norman and friends at the Proper Cafe. I have asked Nicole Dean to express my sympathy to you and your family, and if I can do anything at all to help you and your family through this difficult time, please don't hesitate to call. Norman was a wonderful man who greeted everyone with an award-winning smile, open arms and an unforgettable hug. He was loved by all, and he will truly be missed. You and your family are in my thoughts and prayers. God bless you!

Sonya Breland
Hollywood, Florida

It is with deepest sympathy that I offer my condolences for the loss of your dear brother and our wonderful friend. Norman is, in my opinion, the king of disco. He never missed a beat. Even when I didn't attend the parties for a period of time, he always made me feel welcome with a big smile, a big kiss, an even bigger hug and with sincerity he would say, "I'm so glad you came out tonight; save me a dance."

Just know that he is still loved, and you and your family are in my prayers during this difficult time.

With love,
Kandi Williams

EPILOGUE—MOVING ON

Harold, I am so sorry to hear about Norman. I currently live in VA and Linda Waymer called to inform me about Norman. I will keep checking this site to see when services will be held.

I am hoping that I can arrange my schedule to attend and say goodbye to my good friend, who I would not have had any social life without. I hope you are holding up well, and I will keep you in my prayers.

I am hoping that I will get to see you at the services. If not, please know that I love you and will keep you uplifted.

I am hoping that you can send an address to my personal email address so that I can acknowledge your brother by sending a loving gift.

Carolyn Thomas

We were so saddened to learn of Norman's death. My boyfriend and I know him from La Maganette and he was such a warm, "feel good" kind of person. He was also the perfect "host" at his parties ... always trying to make people feel at ease and just have a good time "hanging out" ... He will be sorely missed. Our deepest sympathies on your loss. If you get a chance, we would like to have the address so that we can send a condolence card. Thank you.

Sincerely,
Berdine Abler and Edwardo De Leon
Take care.

THE DOW TWINS' LEGACY

To the Dow family,

I would like to express my deepest sympathy to the Dow family. The Dow Twins and the parties at Leviticus and Othello are a very important part of my past. I don't know the gentleman personally, but I do know I have a lot of fond memories. So, I say to you, remember the good times and memories. This will keep Norman in our minds and hearts forever.

God bless you all during this difficult time.

Sincerely,
Diane Waithe

Sorry to hear of your loss. I am the Director of Alumni Development at Christ the King High School. We will remember Norman at our Memorial Mass.

On Sunday, November 20th, 2005, at 10:00 a.m., Christ the King Regional High School will celebrate its Annual Memorial Mass. This "Feast Day of Christ the King" makes it possible for alumni, families, friends and past and present faculty to come together at Christ the King to pray for all of those in our CK family who have gone to their eternal rest. The names of all departed alumni, faculty, staff and friends have been entered in the Christ the King Book of Remembrance and will be read out at our service. We hope that all members of the CK community will unite with us as we think of and pray for our dearly loved deceased. Our Memorial Mass will immediately be followed by a complimentary communion breakfast.

To make accommodations for our Day of Remembrance, we request that you RSVP by November 17th, 2005. Everyone is invited to attend. For further information, please contact our Alumni Development Office.

Unfortunately for me, I did not have the pleasure of meeting you and your brother at the November event. I had just found out about your organization a couple of months prior. It was obvious to me that night that you guys were loved and appreciated, and that you do things on a grand scale with class and style. And now, as I have become a part of your email family and have perused your website, I also see that your hearts and souls are/were on the pulse of the community. I was deeply saddened by your brother's death and will continue to hope for peace and comfort in the memories, and the strength to continue to be and do all that is good in this life.

Rochelle Primas

When asked about the service by those unable to attend, I used one word, majestic, which is the best description I can offer. I told them I was taken back to another era: when the males of the tribe, elders and young men attended the ceremony of honoring and funeralizing one of their own, a fallen prince. My heart was filled with joy and pride observing these Black men take charge, which undoubtedly took an enormous burden off the remaining prince. Not negating the women of the tribe, but letting it be known without a doubt the enormity of the love and respect they have for The Dow Twins.

Blessings to all,
Margie

My most heartfelt sympathies to Harold and family on the passing of your brother and son. Being a twin myself, I could not imagine the loss of my other half. Stay strong, Harold. God bless Norman. May he watch over you and your family in your time of need.

Always in our thoughts,
Kenneth and Shirley O'Banyoun

Harold,

Just a short note to convey my deepest sympathies to you and your family. You both are responsible for many good times that my friends and I have had, both past and present … from Justine's, the Intrepid, ski parties in Vail, and the Copa. Norman will be missed. I pray that God gives you and yours the strength to hold up during this difficult time. Stay strong brother … stay strong.

Sincerely,
Lee Lawton

EPILOGUE—MOVING ON

My deepest condolences to Harold and the family. I have shared the news with many native New Yorkers here in the Atlanta area. Many are shocked and saddened by this loss. I have been a devoted follower over the years, beginning with my trip to Cherry Hill, New Jersey to see the Spinners.

Cherish the fond memories, as many of us will. <u>God</u> needed someone who could get a real party started in <u>Heaven</u> and called on <u>Norman</u>.

Fondly,
Sandy Franco from the ATL

Our deepest condolences to the Dow Family.

Norman was a treasure and will be greatly missed; he is in our thoughts and prayers, God Bless!

Linda, Dianna, David Russell
Saint Albans / Annapolis, MD

Please accept my deepest sympathy on the home-going of Norman. I was a former schoolmate and neighbor in Jamaica and attended St. Catherine's with Norman and Harold. I currently reside in North Carolina and recently heard of the sad news.

May you find comfort in our Lord at this very difficult time?

God Bless,
Charleen Cofield-Evans

Harold:

As you can imagine, I was devastated by the news of Norman's passing. All that runs through my mind is, no more Harold and Norman ... you two were inseparable and often thought of as a unit. I'm sure that is weighing on your mind as well. Please know that although you have lost your partner, you still have friends that are here to love and support you. None of us can replace Norman, but if you need anything, please don't hesitate to call.

Sincerely, Joyce Brown

I am very sorry to hear about the passing of Norman. I met Norman and Harold in Mexico in the '70s. We had the greatest time. I try to come out to at least one party yearly to reunite with The Twins and friends of the past.

I will miss Norman's smiling face and dancing a little salsa with him.

God bless your family.

Sincerely,
Cheryl Weller

God is getting ready to throw the biggest bash to welcome home his saints. Perhaps he needed a fun-loving person who could help him with this plan. He perhaps wants a person with wit and charm, a person known to do the job with joy and grace. He wanted someone that understood and was loved by everyone.

I guess he saw it fit to choose the best—Norman.

May God's blessings continue with his family and loved ones.

My husband Reginald and I had been longtime regulars at the Proper Café, going back several years. It was always a pleasure to see Norman standing at the doorway whenever we came into The Proper. Seeing his face had been such a comfort, as he always made my husband and I feel right at home. The Proper Café had been like a home to us; seeing the same familiar faces gave me a feeling no other place could ever replace.

I am still trying to get past his death, knowing that I will never see his warm, friendly smile again. I would look forward to putting my arms around him as I often referred to him lovingly, as a cute "teddy bear." I am amazed, stunned and trying to let my psyche accept that he is gone. I will always love you, Norman ... see you in heaven.

Charlene and Reginald Wade

Hard to believe that I have known them for sixty-plus years. Our families and many of our friends have gone on. Norman will forever be missed and Harold, to this day, is a dear friend. Good friends are like stars. You can't always see them, but they are always there.

Barbara, lifelong friend

THE DOW TWINS' LEGACY

FAREWELL NORMAN by Tony Jenkins

Heartfelt condolences go out to Harold A. Dow and the Dow family for the loss of our fellow SnoBurner Norman Dow. The SnoBurner Ski Club is proud to have had Norman as an honored member for many years.

I met Harold and Norman many years ago, as many of us did through their events giving ... you know ... "Ain't no party like a Dow Twins Party"! But I got to know them and become friends with them through various club activities, mainly skiing. As identical twins, nobody could ever distinguish Harold from Norman or Norman from Harold with any amount of certainty, and it was no different on the slopes. You're riding the ski lift ... a Dow on the left, a Dow on the right ... now, did Norman have on the purple SnoBurner jacket or was it Harold? Or did Harold have the red and white jacket with the black trim? Everybody who knows them knows exactly what I'm saying!

Yeah, I've heard most of the "Which Dow Is It?" clues. My personal favorite was "Harold hair... Norman ... no hair!" Lord help us if Norman decided not to shave one day. Besides, a lot of good that would do when they have ski masks on! But with all the similarities, the most important thing was that they were both "good people."

There were differences ... subtle though they were. If you were heading down a trail with bumps the size of Volkswagens and there's a Dow with you, chances are ... it wasn't Norman! If you're trying to make your way

EPILOGUE—MOVING ON

through some trees off trails and there's a Dow behind you, there again, it probably wasn't Norman! But now if you're sitting around watching TV and a Dow is holding the remote stopped at Formula One Racing, that probably was Norman. Or if a salsa record was pumping out of the speakers at an Aprés Ski party and a Dow was out on the floor getting his swerve on ... that, too, was probably Norman.

As much as they were alike, they were also different, but it will be through Norman's absence that we will see Harold, even as we will always be reminded by him of Norman. We at the SnoBurners have lost a fellow skier and good friend. We the Black community have lost a good man and an icon. We will all miss Norman Dow.

"Norman may your last run be on a never-ending blue trail called peace, at a snow-covered mountain named heavenly."

We at the SnoBurners lost this writer, skier, family man and friend, Tony Jenkins, on November 27th, 2022.

Norman Dow's funeral

Norman's Three Afterlife "Appearances"

The condolence messages we received revolved around a single theme—that Norman wasn't really "gone," but lived on in everyone's hearts. Well, I'm here to tell you that he did more than live on in our hearts—his spirit made itself known to us on several uncanny occasions after his death.

The first "encounter" happened when I and my co-worker at WWRL, Big Al (as I used to call him) went to get lunch at a deli on Seventh Avenue as usual. As we entered the deli, an older Black lady was coming out, so I held the door open for her. She looked at me and started screaming inexplicably and ran down the block.

To say I was shocked would be putting it lightly. I was mortified and embarrassed to say the least. Big Al, who was about 6' 5" feet tall, was watching from behind me and he doubled over in laughter. "I think that lady thought you were your brother come back to life," he explained to me. "The sun was bright and shining from above you, so it looked like you had a halo." I realized then that she looked familiar—she was one of Norman's ticket sellers. The poor woman. But, of course, my brother does live on in me.

The second spiritual encounter with Norman occurred a couple of weeks after his passing at The Proper Café, just before the restaurant opened. Herman Davis, who would open for us on occasion, was sitting near the door in the dining room (where Norman normally sat) watching the wall-mounted television above the bar.

On this day, he was joined by our bartender, Collin, and by Duke, a regular, who turned the TV channel to the basketball game they wanted to watch. The moment the game came on, the TV switched channels to the football game that Norman usually watched.

EPILOGUE—MOVING ON

Friends honoring Norman Dow's life

Norman Dow's funeral

THE DOW TWINS' LEGACY

Norman Dow's funeral

Twenty-six flower arrangements were featured
around the Greater Allen A.M.E. Cathedral

EPILOGUE—MOVING ON

A little surprised by the TV glitch, Herman switched it back to basketball game. Again, the channel changed instantly back to the football game. Well, Duke was having none of it. He screamed, "Norman's here!" and then, "I'm outta here." Duke had no tolerance for ghosts—even if it was his pal Norman.

With Herman's laughter following him, Duke ran down the block, not to be seen at the restaurant for weeks. Totally true story.

Norman made his presence known a third time at one of our many venues, La Maganette restaurant in Midtown East. It had been one of Norman's favorite hangouts during the week, with salsa afterwork on Wednesdays and disco afterwork on Fridays. The manager and he were great friends. Norman even stopped by for dinner before dancing on occasion.

So, when the manager heard of Norman's passing, he was very upset. He had already booked our annual holiday party, which was weeks away, and called to see if it was still on. Justice and I spoke to him and assured him that the event had not been canceled.

On the evening of the party, La Maganette was very busy. Justice and I were welcoming folks into the downstairs area when the manager came flying out of his office. "Norman's here!" he said, breathlessly. "He was just in my office!" He stopped himself mid-sentence when he realized that the place was filled with people and they, Justice and I were all standing there watching him.

After he calmed down, he explained with all sincerity that Norman had appeared in front of his desk. It was shocking, but we knew him well and had no reason to doubt his word. Justice and I imagined that Norman came to dance with his people one last time.

In fact, Norman's presence in our lives in those days following the funeral was predicted by an elderly grandmother who I met at the OTB. She told me, "Norman will be around until he thinks everything is fine and eventually, he'll move on." She was right.

Losing Mom

My mother never really got over Norman's passing (and I tear up myself whenever I speak of him, even now). Mom herself died just a few years later in 2011. The size of the Dow family in the house at the corner of One Hundred Fifteenth Avenue and 168th Street in Queens had dwindled from five people to one.

Mom's passing really hit me; not long after her funeral, my friend Gail Edwards went shopping with me on a Saturday morning as I did every week. Normally, I would have my mom's shopping list along with my own. When I'd headed to the checkout counter of my favorite cashier, Stacey, she would help me separate mom's groceries from mine and then ring up the two orders.

When I came this time with just one order, she asked. "Where's Mom's order?" Tears started running down my face, and I couldn't answer. My friend Gail had to explain, "She passed."

I miss my mother and my brother every day, but I know they are looking out for me, especially because of the number of surgeries and recoveries I've survived against all odds since their passing. I can hear them saying, "We've got it covered up here, Harold. Just do the do down there till later, when we'll see you again."

EPILOGUE—MOVING ON

Mrs. Evelyn Dow at Thanksgiving dinner with Gail Edwards

As I write this, I am reminded how much influence my mom had on me and on those in my circle of friends. Being a Gemini, like her boys, she loved people. She was a great person to be around and a good listener, whether you were just talking about her hobbies like knitting or crocheting, or about life experiences. Her girlfriends were the biggest part of her life, before and after our father's passing, and they spent so much time with her in our home.

For these and many other reasons, the house was symbolic of my mom and her wonderful existence. So, when it came time to release the property to someone else, I knew it was important to whom I sold our family's home. I imagined a young family with children and a dog, since we had a large yard and had grown up with a dog ourselves.

Some folks didn't want me to sell. They wanted me to keep the Dow family corner property but with five trees, a double driveway, and a one-hundred-by-fifty-foot lot, I said *hell no*. Who's going to rake up the leaves of five trees and shovel the snow of a corner house with a double garage? *Not me*. I was fast becoming a senior citizen, at sixty years old at the time. So, The Dow / Sims Estate was now "FOR SALE."

Having made this decision, my next thoughts turned to clearing out a house that still held the belongings of five adults, two office moves, and sixty-two years of memorabilia. I set as my first goal to sell some of Mom's precious items. I could use the proceeds to raise scholarship funds. Listing many items over three weekends was an interesting and rewarding project considering the number of folks that stopped by and bought items. The goal was reached, and I was able to raise $6,000 for scholarships in our family's name for two more worthy students.

After that, my efforts were geared towards giving away everything else—bedroom sets, furniture, my mom's tea sets, handmade quilts, and numerous clothing items—to clear the house for selling. I also had to sift through and shred thousands of documents and stuff mountains of debris into dozens of garbage bags.

Fortunately, I knew my sanitation guys well because they hung out at The Proper Café. They told me not to bother with a private hauling service. Instead, they agreed to take everything away as long as I didn't overload the bags and only put six out at a time—which really meant twelve, since the corner house had a trash pickup on the street side and on the avenue side. It was a win-win situation that required no dumpster rental.

Once all of that was done, my real estate agent, David Lucas, listed the house on a Thursday and had a commitment in writing by Sunday morning (he had a list of folks looking for just such a home in Jamaica). As I'd hoped, the house went to a lovely young couple with three kids and a dog. I knew my mom was thrilled in Heaven above because they loved the house as much as she did. The family added new white fencing, eliminated a couple of trees, and remodeled the interior to their taste.

Meanwhile, I moved to Rochdale Village—the site of Norman and my first professional party. Talk about coming full circle.

Moving On

On March 14th, 2018, I suffered an aortic dissection, just as Norman had in 2005. I was rushed to North Shore Hospital, and thanks to the great staff and doctors, my aorta was repaired in time (with literally minutes to spare). With time, care and rest I fully recovered. I've since had two knee and leg surgeries, but have been blessed to bounce back from each and can now play tennis again (smile).

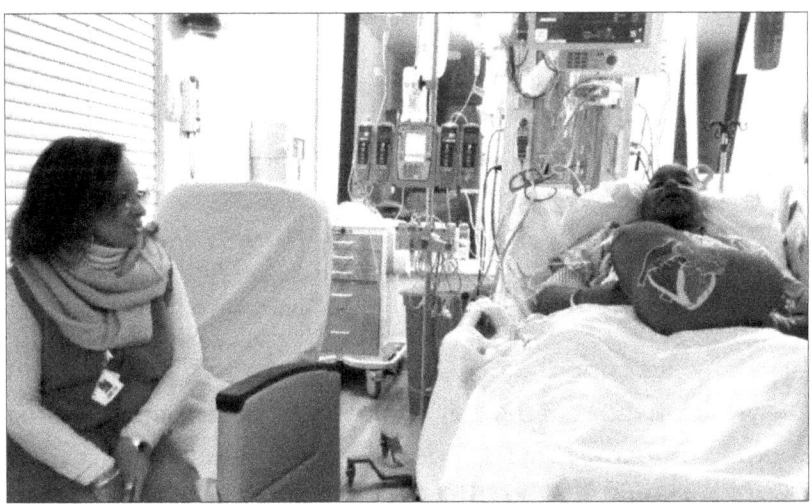

Recuperating from aorta heart surgery with longtime friend Justice at my side

Life has been good for me since moving to a beautiful coop apartment in Rochdale Village. The coop development is well-maintained, which means no heavy lifting is required of me (per my doctor's orders after my surgeries). I've retired from events planning, except for the Day at The Races at Belmont Racetrack, which still happens every Father's Day with record attendance—but that's it. I just pay my rent and keep my heart strong by walking 10,000+ steps a day or playing tennis with friends.

Even during the pandemic from 2019 to 2022, when most folks were sequestered in their homes or apartments protecting themselves from getting infected by others, I was able to venture out each day onto the 120-acre coop property: firstly, to get some fresh air in my system and secondly, to see and greet my many friends and neighbors—even if from a safe distance. By walking the 2.5 miles around the Rochdale Village complex along the inner edge of the street, facing the on-coming traffic, I was within speaking distance of anyone on the sidewalk.

The amount of folks that I met daily was enough to keep my spirits high during that period. Even friends and neighbors who were driving by would honk their horns or pullover to say hello. Life truly is *good*, and I have been blessed.

This has been the story of The Dow Twins, and of my journey with my brother, told for posterity. It's also the story of a generation of young, up-and-coming Black people who began by pursuing their education, then finding their place in the workforce and in the world; and, most of all, enjoying each other's company, camaraderie, friendships and support for a lifetime. Hopefully, its telling will help generations that follow to build strong families and make powerful friendships.

EPILOGUE—MOVING ON

Now, as I come to the end of my chronicle of so many wonderful times with family, friends and supporters throughout the years, I wonder what my next chapter will be. Something wonderful, I'm sure. Thank you to everyone.

Much Love,
Harold

APPENDIX

Classic Dow Twins flyer

THE DOW TWINS' LEGACY

Mike Armstrong

THE POWER COMPANY

Norman Dow, Bob Belle, Harold Dow and Harold Stancil (as shown above left to right) are principals of the Power Company.

All successful businessmen in their own right, they decided their combined efforts would be a power-ful force to reckon with. Thus they became the Power Company.

They have added their personal touch to such posh places as The Palladium, Visage, the Red Parrot and the most unique "The U.S.S. Intrepid." In an effort to give something back to the community which has continually supported them, they have generously donated their time and talents to charitable organizations.

Please accept this invitation to another spectacular event brought to you by the Power Company.

New Year's Eve Extravaganza
Tuesday, December 31, 1985
at
ROEBLING'S
South Street Seaport
Fulton and Water St. (Wall Street area)
Manhattan's historical waterfront district

Live entertainment, hot & cold hors d'oeuvres before midnight. Oldies but goodies, latin and current R&B sounds for your dancing pleasure. Hats, masks, noisemakers and other party favors plus... surprise raffle prizes (including trips)

Advance tickets $25 before December 25th
$35 after, more at door
Fashionable attire

Tickets available at:

Justine's Cabaret, 500 Eighth Ave. (between 35th & 36th St.) Call the Dow Twins (212) 695-9229 1-6 pm Mon. thru Fri.

Fiorucci's, 125 East 59th Street, lower level "sweet B" Call Harold of D.H. Productions (212) 924-4440 9-5 pm Mon thru Fri

70 West, 208 West 70th St. (Wednesday nights only!) Call Bob Belle (718) 429-2727 before 10 pm Mon thru Fri

---

The Power Company & Friends presents

REUNION

Thursday February 13th, 1986
5:30 PM until 2:00 AM

860 BROADWAY
(Near 17th Street)

—**Dance Music Appreciation**—
Oldies-n-Goodies plus Contemporary Music

Class Reunion of 1962 to 1969

We'll "SHING-A-LING" and Grind to sounds from our days in High School and Back-Seat Romances.
Wear something from the '50's or '60's. (letter sweater, black & white bucks, etc)
PRIZES FOR THE BEST OUTFITS!
So try something different, come and bring a friend, a lover, a co-worker or just yourself and meet someone new!
Ten Dollars In Advance
(Fifteen at the door)

TICKETS AVAILABLE AT:

FIORUCCI, 125 East 59th Street, lower level, "Sweet B". Call Harold of D.H. Prod. (212) 924-4440—9:00 AM to 5:00 PM

JUSTINE'S CABARET, 500 Eighth Ave., (between 35 & 36th Sts). Call the Dow Twins (212) 695-9229—1:00 to 6:00 PM; M-F

BRAZIL, BRAZIL, 50 West 77th St. (Friday Nights Only). Call Bob Belle (212) 695-3631, (Beeper)

APPENDIX

12 WEST 21st (between 5th & 6th St.) for Birthday Parties • (212) 534-5742

THURSDAY Afterwork, MAY 1, 1986
6 p.m.-until and Every Thursday thereafter

We have reserved a chic and avant garde video club, featuring top entertainers, for our most discriminating members.

Admission: $5.00 before 8 a.m. with invite — $7.00 after til closing.
— Enjoy the hottest Music Videos on 34 monitors —
Jackets required — Proof of 25 is a must

Hosted by: Herman M and The Dow Twins

Obba Babatunde
Actor, Singer, Dancer, Choreographer

Tony, nominated for his portrayal of C.C. White in the Broadway smash "Dreamgirls", and who plays smooth Rusty Bennett on ABC's "All My Children", will perform his cabaret act.
Showtime: Midnight

POWER COMPANY & Friends
DOW TWINS • D.H. PRODUCTIONS • BOB BELLE
Remember...Red Parrot • Roeblings I, II, III • Palladium I, II
Underground • Intrepid I, II • Limelight • Pier 17

Saturday, December 27, 1986
10 P.M. til

"Christmas/Pre-New Years Affair"
Official Reception For United Negro College Fund
Lou Rawls Telethon-LIVE TELECAST Before Midnight
at the **OMNI PARK CENTRAL** (7 Ave. at 55 St.)
$25 in advance ($20 before Dec. 20th & more at the door)

*Enjoy the sounds of Dr. Bert Morgan
Spinning Contemporary, Salsa and Oldies*

Sponsored By DeKuyper's Peachtree Schnapps

THE DOW TWINS' LEGACY

APPENDIX

EL GRAN COMBO
DE PUERTO RICO
LIVE-N-DANCEABLE

ADMIT · ONE

SUNDAY EVENING APRIL 29th

THE RED PARROT
617 West 57th St. (Bet. 11th & 12th)

5:30 PM till Midnight
Fifteen Dollars ($15.) in advance
Showtime: 7:30 & 9:30 PM
For info & tickets call:
695-9231. • 1-6 PM, Mon.-Fri.

With their hits: EL MENU
EL TELEFONO • LA SOLEDAD
LA MUERTE • ANNIVERSARIO
and many, many more...
*N.Y.'s Largest Wooden Dance Floor

Produced and Sponsored by

 BLS 107.5fm    BURGER KING 149th St. and Melrose Ave. Bronx, N.Y.   Justine's Salsa Fridays

---

THE PARTNERS
THE DOW TWINS • AL FLORANT & ASSOC. • GREG SMITH & CO.
PRESENT

BACK BY POPULAR DEMAND

THE GRAND FINALE
FOR 1992
AT THE SEAPORT

★★★★★★★★★★★★★★★
SPECIAL DISCOUNT OFFER
Special For All Those Celebrating Their
SAGITTARIAN
Birthdays With Friends!
A Discount Price Will Be Available
With The Purchase Of 10 Or More
Advance Tickets Before November 21st
Call For Further Information.
★★★★★★★★★★★★★★★

THE MUSEUM CLUB
AT BRIDGEWATERS COMPLEX
11 Fulton Street • South Street Seaport
Atop the Fulton Street Market Building
New York City

THANKSGIVING WEEKEND
Saturday Night, November 28th • 10 pm-4 am

- Explosive Dance Music & Discotizer Prod.
- Live Reggae Music by "TOP SECRET"
- Hilarious Comedy Revue by Non-Stop Prod.
- Reminisce with the recorded sounds of Oldies 'n Goodies

Admission: $10 before November 21st
Attire: Dress Fashionable

For Travel Directions & Information
(212) 695-7643

HOSTED BY THE PARTNERS:
Greg Smith, Al Florant, The Dow Twins, Hook,
Henry Lanclos, John Taylor and Dan Byrd

APPENDIX

APPENDIX

Many thanks to the following photographers, who documented many of our activities over fifty years:

    Arnett Murray
    Gerald Peart
    Robert Cave
    Alix DeJean
    Jimmy Coles
    Harold & Norman Dow
    Tracey Mc Allister
    Bruce Moore
    Kwame Brathwaite
    Allen Morgan
    Ron Warner

www.ingramcontent.com/pod-product-compliance
Lightning Source LLC
Chambersburg PA
CBHW050253010526
44107CB00003B/303